C-3272 CAREER EXAMINATION SERIES

This is your PASSBOOK for...

Clerk II

Test Preparation Study Guide
Questions & Answers

NLC®

NATIONAL LEARNING CORPORATION®

National Learning Corporation

212 Michael Drive, Syosset, NY 11791
(516) 921-8888 • www.passbooks.com
E-mail: info@passbooks.com

PUBLISHED IN THE UNITED STATES OF AMERICA

PASSBOOK® SERIES

THE *PASSBOOK® SERIES* has been created to prepare applicants and candidates for the ultimate academic battlefield – the examination room.

At some time in our lives, each and every one of us may be required to take an examination – for validation, matriculation, admission, qualification, registration, certification, or licensure.

Based on the assumption that every applicant or candidate has met the basic formal educational standards, has taken the required number of courses, and read the necessary texts, the *PASSBOOK® SERIES* furnishes the one special preparation which may assure passing with confidence, instead of failing with insecurity. Examination questions – together with answers – are furnished as the basic vehicle for study so that the mysteries of the examination and its compounding difficulties may be eliminated or diminished by a sure method.

This book is meant to help you pass your examination provided that you qualify and are serious in your objective.

The entire field is reviewed through the huge store of content information which is succinctly presented through a provocative and challenging approach – the question-and-answer method.

A climate of success is established by furnishing the correct answers at the end of each test.

You soon learn to recognize types of questions, forms of questions, and patterns of questioning. You may even begin to anticipate expected outcomes.

You perceive that many questions are repeated or adapted so that you can gain acute insights, which may enable you to score many sure points.

You learn how to confront new questions, or types of questions, and to attack them confidently and work out the correct answers.

You note objectives and emphases, and recognize pitfalls and dangers, so that you may make positive educational adjustments.

Moreover, you are kept fully informed in relation to new concepts, methods, practices, and directions in the field.

You discover that you are actually taking the examination all the time: you are preparing for the examination by "taking" an examination, not by reading extraneous and/or supererogatory textbooks.

In short, this PASSBOOK®, used directedly, should be an important factor in helping you to pass your test.

CLERK II

DUTIES:

This is clerical work involving the independent performance of higher level clerical tasks which may include contact with the public or handling of funds. Assignments given to employees in this class involve little or no typing. The work is performed in accordance with general instructions regarding objectives, policies and procedures. The work is not subject to detailed or immediate review and is usually in its completed form. Employees of this class may exercise supervision or guidance over a small number of clerks and may train a small number of clerks in the procedures used for that section. General supervision is received from a higher level employee who is available to handle more difficult or technical problems. Performs related work as required.

TYPICAL WORK ACTIVITIES:

- Enters information onto standard forms such as payroll or production records, authorizations and certifications;
- Maintains records of monetary, budgetary or similar transactions;
- Compiles arithmetic summaries and reports;
- Prepares and maintains written communications such as memos, reports, and related tables, listings and charts that require familiarity with section procedures and policies;
- Prepares and maintains alphabetical and numerical files;
- Searches files, records and references for information;
- Prepares written documents, certifications, authorizations, and forms;
- Obtains and gives out information by telephone, correspondence, or in person;
- May supervise, guide, or train subordinates in the performance of their duties;
- May compute interest, taxes and price extensions.

SUBJECT OF EXAMINATION:

The written test is designed to evaluate knowledge, skills and/or abilities in the following areas:

1. **Coding/Decoding Information** — These questions test for the ability to follow a set of coding rules. Some questions will require you to code information by converting certain information into letters or numbers. Other questions will require you to decode information by determining if the information that has already been converted into letters or numbers is correct. Complete directions will be provided; no previous knowledge of or training in any coding system is required.
2. **Name and Number Checking** — These questions test for the ability to distinguish between sets of words, letters, and/or numbers that are almost exactly alike. Material is usually presented in two or three columns, and you will have to determine how the entry in the first column compares with the entry in the second column and possibly the third. You will be instructed to mark your answers according to a designated code provided in the directions.
3. **Office Record Keeping** — These questions test your ability to perform common office record keeping tasks. The test consists of two or more "sets" of questions, each set concerning a different problem. Typical record keeping problems might involve the organization or collation of data from several sources; scheduling; maintaining a record system using running balances; or completion of a table summarizing data using totals, subtotals, averages and percents.
4. **Operations with Letters and Numbers** — These questions test for skills and abilities in operations involving alphabetizing, comparing, checking and counting. The questions require you to follow the specific directions given for each question which may involve alphabetizing, comparing, checking and counting given groups of letters and/or numbers.

HOW TO TAKE A TEST

I. YOU MUST PASS AN EXAMINATION

A. WHAT EVERY CANDIDATE SHOULD KNOW

Examination applicants often ask us for help in preparing for the written test. What can I study in advance? What kinds of questions will be asked? How will the test be given? How will the papers be graded?

As an applicant for a civil service examination, you may be wondering about some of these things. Our purpose here is to suggest effective methods of advance study and to describe civil service examinations.

Your chances for success on this examination can be increased if you know how to prepare. Those "pre-examination jitters" can be reduced if you know what to expect. You can even experience an adventure in good citizenship if you know why civil service exams are given.

B. WHY ARE CIVIL SERVICE EXAMINATIONS GIVEN?

Civil service examinations are important to you in two ways. As a citizen, you want public jobs filled by employees who know how to do their work. As a job seeker, you want a fair chance to compete for that job on an equal footing with other candidates. The best-known means of accomplishing this two-fold goal is the competitive examination.

Exams are widely publicized throughout the nation. They may be administered for jobs in federal, state, city, municipal, town or village governments or agencies.

Any citizen may apply, with some limitations, such as the age or residence of applicants. Your experience and education may be reviewed to see whether you meet the requirements for the particular examination. When these requirements exist, they are reasonable and applied consistently to all applicants. Thus, a competitive examination may cause you some uneasiness now, but it is your privilege and safeguard.

C. HOW ARE CIVIL SERVICE EXAMS DEVELOPED?

Examinations are carefully written by trained technicians who are specialists in the field known as "psychological measurement," in consultation with recognized authorities in the field of work that the test will cover. These experts recommend the subject matter areas or skills to be tested; only those knowledges or skills important to your success on the job are included. The most reliable books and source materials available are used as references. Together, the experts and technicians judge the difficulty level of the questions.

Test technicians know how to phrase questions so that the problem is clearly stated. Their ethics do not permit "trick" or "catch" questions. Questions may have been tried out on sample groups, or subjected to statistical analysis, to determine their usefulness.

Written tests are often used in combination with performance tests, ratings of training and experience, and oral interviews. All of these measures combine to form the best-known means of finding the right person for the right job.

II. HOW TO PASS THE WRITTEN TEST

A. NATURE OF THE EXAMINATION

To prepare intelligently for civil service examinations, you should know how they differ from school examinations you have taken. In school you were assigned certain definite pages to read or subjects to cover. The examination questions were quite detailed and usually emphasized memory. Civil service exams, on the other hand, try to discover your present ability to perform the duties of a position, plus your potentiality to learn these duties. In other words, a civil service exam attempts to predict how successful you will be. Questions cover such a broad area that they cannot be as minute and detailed as school exam questions.

In the public service similar kinds of work, or positions, are grouped together in one "class." This process is known as *position-classification.* All the positions in a class are paid according to the salary range for that class. One class title covers all of these positions, and they are all tested by the same examination.

B. FOUR BASIC STEPS

1) Study the announcement

How, then, can you know what subjects to study? Our best answer is: "Learn as much as possible about the class of positions for which you've applied." The exam will test the knowledge, skills and abilities needed to do the work.

Your most valuable source of information about the position you want is the official exam announcement. This announcement lists the training and experience qualifications. Check these standards and apply only if you come reasonably close to meeting them.

The brief description of the position in the examination announcement offers some clues to the subjects which will be tested. Think about the job itself. Review the duties in your mind. Can you perform them, or are there some in which you are rusty? Fill in the blank spots in your preparation.

Many jurisdictions preview the written test in the exam announcement by including a section called "Knowledge and Abilities Required," "Scope of the Examination," or some similar heading. Here you will find out specifically what fields will be tested.

2) Review your own background

Once you learn in general what the position is all about, and what you need to know to do the work, ask yourself which subjects you already know fairly well and which need improvement. You may wonder whether to concentrate on improving your strong areas or on building some background in your fields of weakness. When the announcement has specified "some knowledge" or "considerable knowledge," or has used adjectives like "beginning principles of..." or "advanced ... methods," you can get a clue as to the number and difficulty of questions to be asked in any given field. More questions, and hence broader coverage, would be included for those subjects which are more important in the work. Now weigh your strengths and weaknesses against the job requirements and prepare accordingly.

3) Determine the level of the position

Another way to tell how intensively you should prepare is to understand the level of the job for which you are applying. Is it the entering level? In other words, is this the position in which beginners in a field of work are hired? Or is it an intermediate or advanced level? Sometimes this is indicated by such words as "Junior" or "Senior" in the class title. Other jurisdictions use Roman numerals to designate the level – Clerk I, Clerk II, for example. The word "Supervisor" sometimes appears in the title. If the level is not indicated by the title, check the description of duties. Will you be working under very close supervision, or will you have responsibility for independent decisions in this work?

4) Choose appropriate study materials

Now that you know the subjects to be examined and the relative amount of each subject to be covered, you can choose suitable study materials. For beginning level jobs, or even advanced ones, if you have a pronounced weakness in some aspect of your training, read a modern, standard textbook in that field. Be sure it is up to date and has general coverage. Such books are normally available at your library, and the librarian will be glad to help you locate one. For entry-level positions, questions of appropriate difficulty are chosen – neither highly advanced questions, nor those too simple. Such questions require careful thought but not advanced training.

If the position for which you are applying is technical or advanced, you will read more advanced, specialized material. If you are already familiar with the basic principles of your field, elementary textbooks would waste your time. Concentrate on advanced textbooks and technical periodicals. Think through the concepts and review difficult problems in your field.

These are all general sources. You can get more ideas on your own initiative, following these leads. For example, training manuals and publications of the government agency which employs workers in your field can be useful, particularly for technical and professional positions. A letter or visit to the government department involved may result in more specific study suggestions, and certainly will provide you with a more definite idea of the exact nature of the position you are seeking.

III. KINDS OF TESTS

Tests are used for purposes other than measuring knowledge and ability to perform specified duties. For some positions, it is equally important to test ability to make adjustments to new situations or to profit from training. In others, basic mental abilities not dependent on information are essential. Questions which test these things may not appear as pertinent to the duties of the position as those which test for knowledge and information. Yet they are often highly important parts of a fair examination. For very general questions, it is almost impossible to help you direct your study efforts. What we can do is to point out some of the more common of these general abilities needed in public service positions and describe some typical questions.

1) General information

Broad, general information has been found useful for predicting job success in some kinds of work. This is tested in a variety of ways, from vocabulary lists to questions about current events. Basic background in some field of work, such as sociology or economics, may be sampled in a group of questions. Often these are principles which have become familiar to most persons through exposure rather than through formal training. It is difficult to advise you how to study for these questions; being alert to the world around you is our best suggestion.

2) Verbal ability

An example of an ability needed in many positions is verbal or language ability. Verbal ability is, in brief, the ability to use and understand words. Vocabulary and grammar tests are typical measures of this ability. Reading comprehension or paragraph interpretation questions are common in many kinds of civil service tests. You are given a paragraph of written material and asked to find its central meaning.

3) Numerical ability

Number skills can be tested by the familiar arithmetic problem, by checking paired lists of numbers to see which are alike and which are different, or by interpreting charts and graphs. In the latter test, a graph may be printed in the test booklet which you are asked to use as the basis for answering questions.

4) Observation

A popular test for law-enforcement positions is the observation test. A picture is shown to you for several minutes, then taken away. Questions about the picture test your ability to observe both details and larger elements.

5) Following directions

In many positions in the public service, the employee must be able to carry out written instructions dependably and accurately. You may be given a chart with several columns, each column listing a variety of information. The questions require you to carry out directions involving the information given in the chart.

6) Skills and aptitudes

Performance tests effectively measure some manual skills and aptitudes. When the skill is one in which you are trained, such as typing or shorthand, you can practice. These tests are often very much like those given in business school or high school courses. For many of the other skills and aptitudes, however, no short-time preparation can be made. Skills and abilities natural to you or that you have developed throughout your lifetime are being tested.

Many of the general questions just described provide all the data needed to answer the questions and ask you to use your reasoning ability to find the answers. Your best preparation for these tests, as well as for tests of facts and ideas, is to be at your physical and mental best. You, no doubt, have your own methods of getting into an exam-taking mood and keeping "in shape." The next section lists some ideas on this subject.

IV. KINDS OF QUESTIONS

Only rarely is the "essay" question, which you answer in narrative form, used in civil service tests. Civil service tests are usually of the short-answer type. Full instructions for answering these questions will be given to you at the examination. But in case this is your first experience with short-answer questions and separate answer sheets, here is what you need to know:

1) Multiple-choice Questions

Most popular of the short-answer questions is the "multiple choice" or "best answer" question. It can be used, for example, to test for factual knowledge, ability to solve problems or judgment in meeting situations found at work.

A multiple-choice question is normally one of three types—

- It can begin with an incomplete statement followed by several possible endings. You are to find the one ending which *best* completes the statement, although some of the others may not be entirely wrong.
- It can also be a complete statement in the form of a question which is answered by choosing one of the statements listed.

- It can be in the form of a problem – again you select the best answer.

Here is an example of a multiple-choice question with a discussion which should give you some clues as to the method for choosing the right answer:

When an employee has a complaint about his assignment, the action which will *best* help him overcome his difficulty is to
A. discuss his difficulty with his coworkers
B. take the problem to the head of the organization
C. take the problem to the person who gave him the assignment
D. say nothing to anyone about his complaint

In answering this question, you should study each of the choices to find which is best. Consider choice "A" – Certainly an employee may discuss his complaint with fellow employees, but no change or improvement can result, and the complaint remains unresolved. Choice "B" is a poor choice since the head of the organization probably does not know what assignment you have been given, and taking your problem to him is known as "going over the head" of the supervisor. The supervisor, or person who made the assignment, is the person who can clarify it or correct any injustice. Choice "C" is, therefore, correct. To say nothing, as in choice "D," is unwise. Supervisors have and interest in knowing the problems employees are facing, and the employee is seeking a solution to his problem.

2) True/False Questions

The "true/false" or "right/wrong" form of question is sometimes used. Here a complete statement is given. Your job is to decide whether the statement is right or wrong.

SAMPLE: A roaming cell-phone call to a nearby city costs less than a non-roaming call to a distant city.

This statement is wrong, or false, since roaming calls are more expensive.

This is not a complete list of all possible question forms, although most of the others are variations of these common types. You will always get complete directions for answering questions. Be sure you understand *how* to mark your answers – ask questions until you do.

V. RECORDING YOUR ANSWERS

Computer terminals are used more and more today for many different kinds of exams.

For an examination with very few applicants, you may be told to record your answers in the test booklet itself. Separate answer sheets are much more common. If this separate answer sheet is to be scored by machine – and this is often the case – it is highly important that you mark your answers correctly in order to get credit.

An electronic scoring machine is often used in civil service offices because of the speed with which papers can be scored. Machine-scored answer sheets must be marked with a pencil, which will be given to you. This pencil has a high graphite content which responds to the electronic scoring machine. As a matter of fact, stray dots may register as answers, so do not let your pencil rest on the answer sheet while you are pondering the correct answer. Also, if your pencil lead breaks or is otherwise defective, ask for another.

Since the answer sheet will be dropped in a slot in the scoring machine, be careful not to bend the corners or get the paper crumpled.

The answer sheet normally has five vertical columns of numbers, with 30 numbers to a column. These numbers correspond to the question numbers in your test booklet. After each number, going across the page are four or five pairs of dotted lines. These short dotted lines have small letters or numbers above them. The first two pairs may also have a "T" or "F" above the letters. This indicates that the first two pairs only are to be used if the questions are of the true-false type. If the questions are multiple choice, disregard the "T" and "F" and pay attention only to the small letters or numbers.

Answer your questions in the manner of the sample that follows:

32. The largest city in the United States is
    - A. Washington, D.C.
    - B. New York City
    - C. Chicago
    - D. Detroit
    - E. San Francisco

1) Choose the answer you think is best. (New York City is the largest, so "B" is correct.)
2) Find the row of dotted lines numbered the same as the question you are answering. (Find row number 32)
3) Find the pair of dotted lines corresponding to the answer. (Find the pair of lines under the mark "B.")
4) Make a solid black mark between the dotted lines.

VI. BEFORE THE TEST

Common sense will help you find procedures to follow to get ready for an examination. Too many of us, however, overlook these sensible measures. Indeed, nervousness and fatigue have been found to be the most serious reasons why applicants fail to do their best on civil service tests. Here is a list of reminders:

- Begin your preparation early – Don't wait until the last minute to go scurrying around for books and materials or to find out what the position is all about.
- Prepare continuously – An hour a night for a week is better than an all-night cram session. This has been definitely established. What is more, a night a week for a month will return better dividends than crowding your study into a shorter period of time.
- Locate the place of the exam – You have been sent a notice telling you when and where to report for the examination. If the location is in a different town or otherwise unfamiliar to you, it would be well to inquire the best route and learn something about the building.
- Relax the night before the test – Allow your mind to rest. Do not study at all that night. Plan some mild recreation or diversion; then go to bed early and get a good night's sleep.
- Get up early enough to make a leisurely trip to the place for the test – This way unforeseen events, traffic snarls, unfamiliar buildings, etc. will not upset you.
- Dress comfortably – A written test is not a fashion show. You will be known by number and not by name, so wear something comfortable.

- Leave excess paraphernalia at home – Shopping bags and odd bundles will get in your way. You need bring only the items mentioned in the official notice you received; usually everything you need is provided. Do not bring reference books to the exam. They will only confuse those last minutes and be taken away from you when in the test room.
- Arrive somewhat ahead of time – If because of transportation schedules you must get there very early, bring a newspaper or magazine to take your mind off yourself while waiting.
- Locate the examination room – When you have found the proper room, you will be directed to the seat or part of the room where you will sit. Sometimes you are given a sheet of instructions to read while you are waiting. Do not fill out any forms until you are told to do so; just read them and be prepared.
- Relax and prepare to listen to the instructions
- If you have any physical problem that may keep you from doing your best, be sure to tell the test administrator. If you are sick or in poor health, you really cannot do your best on the exam. You can come back and take the test some other time.

VII. AT THE TEST

The day of the test is here and you have the test booklet in your hand. The temptation to get going is very strong. Caution! There is more to success than knowing the right answers. You must know how to identify your papers and understand variations in the type of short-answer question used in this particular examination. Follow these suggestions for maximum results from your efforts:

1) Cooperate with the monitor

The test administrator has a duty to create a situation in which you can be as much at ease as possible. He will give instructions, tell you when to begin, check to see that you are marking your answer sheet correctly, and so on. He is not there to guard you, although he will see that your competitors do not take unfair advantage. He wants to help you do your best.

2) Listen to all instructions

Don't jump the gun! Wait until you understand all directions. In most civil service tests you get more time than you need to answer the questions. So don't be in a hurry. Read each word of instructions until you clearly understand the meaning. Study the examples, listen to all announcements and follow directions. Ask questions if you do not understand what to do.

3) Identify your papers

Civil service exams are usually identified by number only. You will be assigned a number; you must not put your name on your test papers. Be sure to copy your number correctly. Since more than one exam may be given, copy your exact examination title.

4) Plan your time

Unless you are told that a test is a "speed" or "rate of work" test, speed itself is usually not important. Time enough to answer all the questions will be provided, but this does not mean that you have all day. An overall time limit has been set. Divide the total time (in minutes) by the number of questions to determine the approximate time you have for each question.

5) Do not linger over difficult questions

If you come across a difficult question, mark it with a paper clip (useful to have along) and come back to it when you have been through the booklet. One caution if you do this – be sure to skip a number on your answer sheet as well. Check often to be sure that you have not lost your place and that you are marking in the row numbered the same as the question you are answering.

6) Read the questions

Be sure you know what the question asks! Many capable people are unsuccessful because they failed to *read* the questions correctly.

7) Answer all questions

Unless you have been instructed that a penalty will be deducted for incorrect answers, it is better to guess than to omit a question.

8) Speed tests

It is often better NOT to guess on speed tests. It has been found that on timed tests people are tempted to spend the last few seconds before time is called in marking answers at random – without even reading them – in the hope of picking up a few extra points. To discourage this practice, the instructions may warn you that your score will be "corrected" for guessing. That is, a penalty will be applied. The incorrect answers will be deducted from the correct ones, or some other penalty formula will be used.

9) Review your answers

If you finish before time is called, go back to the questions you guessed or omitted to give them further thought. Review other answers if you have time.

10) Return your test materials

If you are ready to leave before others have finished or time is called, take ALL your materials to the monitor and leave quietly. Never take any test material with you. The monitor can discover whose papers are not complete, and taking a test booklet may be grounds for disqualification.

VIII. EXAMINATION TECHNIQUES

1) Read the general instructions carefully. These are usually printed on the first page of the exam booklet. As a rule, these instructions refer to the timing of the examination; the fact that you should not start work until the signal and must stop work at a signal, etc. If there are any *special* instructions, such as a choice of questions to be answered, make sure that you note this instruction carefully.

2) When you are ready to start work on the examination, that is as soon as the signal has been given, read the instructions to each question booklet, underline any key words or phrases, such as *least*, *best*, *outline*, *describe* and the like. In this way you will tend to answer as requested rather than discover on reviewing your paper that you *listed without describing*, that you selected the *worst* choice rather than the *best* choice, etc.

3) If the examination is of the objective or multiple-choice type – that is, each question will also give a series of possible answers: A, B, C or D, and you are called upon to select the best answer and write the letter next to that answer on your answer paper – it is advisable to start answering each question in turn. There may be anywhere from 50 to 100 such questions in the three or four hours allotted and you can see how much time would be taken if you read through all the questions before beginning to answer any. Furthermore, if you come across a question or group of questions which you know would be difficult to answer, it would undoubtedly affect your handling of all the other questions.

4) If the examination is of the essay type and contains but a few questions, it is a moot point as to whether you should read all the questions before starting to answer any one. Of course, if you are given a choice – say five out of seven and the like – then it is essential to read all the questions so you can eliminate the two that are most difficult. If, however, you are asked to answer all the questions, there may be danger in trying to answer the easiest one first because you may find that you will spend too much time on it. The best technique is to answer the first question, then proceed to the second, etc.

5) Time your answers. Before the exam begins, write down the time it started, then add the time allowed for the examination and write down the time it must be completed, then divide the time available somewhat as follows:
   - If 3-1/2 hours are allowed, that would be 210 minutes. If you have 80 objective-type questions, that would be an average of 2-1/2 minutes per question. Allow yourself no more than 2 minutes per question, or a total of 160 minutes, which will permit about 50 minutes to review.
   - If for the time allotment of 210 minutes there are 7 essay questions to answer, that would average about 30 minutes a question. Give yourself only 25 minutes per question so that you have about 35 minutes to review.

6) The most important instruction is to *read each question* and make sure you know what is wanted. The second most important instruction is to *time yourself properly* so that you answer every question. The third most important instruction is to *answer every question*. Guess if you have to but include something for each question. Remember that you will receive no credit for a blank and will probably receive some credit if you write something in answer to an essay question. If you guess a letter – say "B" for a multiple-choice question – you may have guessed right. If you leave a blank as an answer to a multiple-choice question, the examiners may respect your feelings but it will not add a point to your score. Some exams may penalize you for wrong answers, so in such cases *only*, you may not want to guess unless you have some basis for your answer.

7) Suggestions
   a. Objective-type questions
      1. Examine the question booklet for proper sequence of pages and questions
      2. Read all instructions carefully
      3. Skip any question which seems too difficult; return to it after all other questions have been answered
      4. Apportion your time properly; do not spend too much time on any single question or group of questions

5. Note and underline key words – *all, most, fewest, least, best, worst, same, opposite,* etc.
6. Pay particular attention to negatives
7. Note unusual option, e.g., unduly long, short, complex, different or similar in content to the body of the question
8. Observe the use of "hedging" words – *probably, may, most likely,* etc.
9. Make sure that your answer is put next to the same number as the question
10. Do not second-guess unless you have good reason to believe the second answer is definitely more correct
11. Cross out original answer if you decide another answer is more accurate; do not erase until you are ready to hand your paper in
12. Answer all questions; guess unless instructed otherwise
13. Leave time for review

b. Essay questions
1. Read each question carefully
2. Determine exactly what is wanted. Underline key words or phrases.
3. Decide on outline or paragraph answer
4. Include many different points and elements unless asked to develop any one or two points or elements
5. Show impartiality by giving pros and cons unless directed to select one side only
6. Make and write down any assumptions you find necessary to answer the questions
7. Watch your English, grammar, punctuation and choice of words
8. Time your answers; don't crowd material

8) Answering the essay question

Most essay questions can be answered by framing the specific response around several key words or ideas. Here are a few such key words or ideas:

M's: manpower, materials, methods, money, management
P's: purpose, program, policy, plan, procedure, practice, problems, pitfalls, personnel, public relations

a. Six basic steps in handling problems:
1. Preliminary plan and background development
2. Collect information, data and facts
3. Analyze and interpret information, data and facts
4. Analyze and develop solutions as well as make recommendations
5. Prepare report and sell recommendations
6. Install recommendations and follow up effectiveness

b. Pitfalls to avoid
1. *Taking things for granted* – A statement of the situation does not necessarily imply that each of the elements is necessarily true; for example, a complaint may be invalid and biased so that all that can be taken for granted is that a complaint has been registered

2. *Considering only one side of a situation* – Wherever possible, indicate several alternatives and then point out the reasons you selected the best one
3. *Failing to indicate follow up* – Whenever your answer indicates action on your part, make certain that you will take proper follow-up action to see how successful your recommendations, procedures or actions turn out to be
4. *Taking too long in answering any single question* – Remember to time your answers properly

IX. AFTER THE TEST

Scoring procedures differ in detail among civil service jurisdictions although the general principles are the same. Whether the papers are hand-scored or graded by machine we have described, they are nearly always graded by number. That is, the person who marks the paper knows only the number – never the name – of the applicant. Not until all the papers have been graded will they be matched with names. If other tests, such as training and experience or oral interview ratings have been given, scores will be combined. Different parts of the examination usually have different weights. For example, the written test might count 60 percent of the final grade, and a rating of training and experience 40 percent. In many jurisdictions, veterans will have a certain number of points added to their grades.

After the final grade has been determined, the names are placed in grade order and an eligible list is established. There are various methods for resolving ties between those who get the same final grade – probably the most common is to place first the name of the person whose application was received first. Job offers are made from the eligible list in the order the names appear on it. You will be notified of your grade and your rank as soon as all these computations have been made. This will be done as rapidly as possible.

People who are found to meet the requirements in the announcement are called "eligibles." Their names are put on a list of eligible candidates. An eligible's chances of getting a job depend on how high he stands on this list and how fast agencies are filling jobs from the list.

When a job is to be filled from a list of eligibles, the agency asks for the names of people on the list of eligibles for that job. When the civil service commission receives this request, it sends to the agency the names of the three people highest on this list. Or, if the job to be filled has specialized requirements, the office sends the agency the names of the top three persons who meet these requirements from the general list.

The appointing officer makes a choice from among the three people whose names were sent to him. If the selected person accepts the appointment, the names of the others are put back on the list to be considered for future openings.

That is the rule in hiring from all kinds of eligible lists, whether they are for typist, carpenter, chemist, or something else. For every vacancy, the appointing officer has his choice of any one of the top three eligibles on the list. This explains why the person whose name is on top of the list sometimes does not get an appointment when some of the persons lower on the list do. If the appointing officer chooses the second or third eligible, the No. 1 eligible does not get a job at once, but stays on the list until he is appointed or the list is terminated.

X. HOW TO PASS THE INTERVIEW TEST

The examination for which you applied requires an oral interview test. You have already taken the written test and you are now being called for the interview test – the final part of the formal examination.

You may think that it is not possible to prepare for an interview test and that there are no procedures to follow during an interview. Our purpose is to point out some things you can do in advance that will help you and some good rules to follow and pitfalls to avoid while you are being interviewed.

What is an interview supposed to test?

The written examination is designed to test the technical knowledge and competence of the candidate; the oral is designed to evaluate intangible qualities, not readily measured otherwise, and to establish a list showing the relative fitness of each candidate – as measured against his competitors – for the position sought. Scoring is not on the basis of "right" and "wrong," but on a sliding scale of values ranging from "not passable" to "outstanding." As a matter of fact, it is possible to achieve a relatively low score without a single "incorrect" answer because of evident weakness in the qualities being measured.

Occasionally, an examination may consist entirely of an oral test – either an individual or a group oral. In such cases, information is sought concerning the technical knowledges and abilities of the candidate, since there has been no written examination for this purpose. More commonly, however, an oral test is used to supplement a written examination.

Who conducts interviews?

The composition of oral boards varies among different jurisdictions. In nearly all, a representative of the personnel department serves as chairman. One of the members of the board may be a representative of the department in which the candidate would work. In some cases, "outside experts" are used, and, frequently, a businessman or some other representative of the general public is asked to serve. Labor and management or other special groups may be represented. The aim is to secure the services of experts in the appropriate field.

However the board is composed, it is a good idea (and not at all improper or unethical) to ascertain in advance of the interview who the members are and what groups they represent. When you are introduced to them, you will have some idea of their backgrounds and interests, and at least you will not stutter and stammer over their names.

What should be done before the interview?

While knowledge about the board members is useful and takes some of the surprise element out of the interview, there is other preparation which is more substantive. It *is* possible to prepare for an oral interview – in several ways:

1) Keep a copy of your application and review it carefully before the interview

This may be the only document before the oral board, and the starting point of the interview. Know what education and experience you have listed there, and the sequence and dates of all of it. Sometimes the board will ask you to review the highlights of your experience for them; you should not have to hem and haw doing it.

2) Study the class specification and the examination announcement

Usually, the oral board has one or both of these to guide them. The qualities, characteristics or knowledges required by the position sought are stated in these documents. They offer valuable clues as to the nature of the oral interview. For example, if the job involves supervisory responsibilities, the announcement will usually indicate that knowledge of modern supervisory methods and the qualifications of the candidate as a supervisor will be tested. If so, you can expect such questions, frequently in the form of a hypothetical situation which you are expected to solve. NEVER go into an oral without knowledge of the duties and responsibilities of the job you seek.

3) Think through each qualification required

Try to visualize the kind of questions you would ask if you were a board member. How well could you answer them? Try especially to appraise your own knowledge and background in each area, *measured against the job sought*, and identify any areas in which you are weak. Be critical and realistic – do not flatter yourself.

4) Do some general reading in areas in which you feel you may be weak

For example, if the job involves supervision and your past experience has NOT, some general reading in supervisory methods and practices, particularly in the field of human relations, might be useful. Do NOT study agency procedures or detailed manuals. The oral board will be testing your understanding and capacity, not your memory.

5) Get a good night's sleep and watch your general health and mental attitude

You will want a clear head at the interview. Take care of a cold or any other minor ailment, and of course, no hangovers.

What should be done on the day of the interview?

Now comes the day of the interview itself. Give yourself plenty of time to get there. Plan to arrive somewhat ahead of the scheduled time, particularly if your appointment is in the fore part of the day. If a previous candidate fails to appear, the board might be ready for you a bit early. By early afternoon an oral board is almost invariably behind schedule if there are many candidates, and you may have to wait. Take along a book or magazine to read, or your application to review, but leave any extraneous material in the waiting room when you go in for your interview. In any event, relax and compose yourself.

The matter of dress is important. The board is forming impressions about you – from your experience, your manners, your attitude, and your appearance. Give your personal appearance careful attention. Dress your best, but not your flashiest. Choose conservative, appropriate clothing, and be sure it is immaculate. This is a business interview, and your appearance should indicate that you regard it as such. Besides, being well groomed and properly dressed will help boost your confidence.

Sooner or later, someone will call your name and escort you into the interview room. *This is it.* From here on you are on your own. It is too late for any more preparation. But remember, you asked for this opportunity to prove your fitness, and you are here because your request was granted.

What happens when you go in?

The usual sequence of events will be as follows: The clerk (who is often the board stenographer) will introduce you to the chairman of the oral board, who will introduce you to the other members of the board. Acknowledge the introductions before you sit down. Do not be surprised if you find a microphone facing you or a stenotypist sitting by. Oral interviews are usually recorded in the event of an appeal or other review.

Usually the chairman of the board will open the interview by reviewing the highlights of your education and work experience from your application – primarily for the benefit of the other members of the board, as well as to get the material into the record. Do not interrupt or comment unless there is an error or significant misinterpretation; if that is the case, do not hesitate. But do not quibble about insignificant matters. Also, he will usually ask you some question about your education, experience or your present job – partly to get you to start talking and to establish the interviewing "rapport." He may start the actual questioning, or turn it over to one of the other members. Frequently, each member undertakes the questioning on a particular area, one in which he is perhaps most competent, so you can expect each member to participate in the examination. Because time is limited, you may also expect some rather abrupt switches in the direction the questioning takes, so do not be upset by it. Normally, a board member will not pursue a single line of questioning unless he discovers a particular strength or weakness.

After each member has participated, the chairman will usually ask whether any member has any further questions, then will ask you if you have anything you wish to add. Unless you are expecting this question, it may floor you. Worse, it may start you off on an extended, extemporaneous speech. The board is not usually seeking more information. The question is principally to offer you a last opportunity to present further qualifications or to indicate that you have nothing to add. So, if you feel that a significant qualification or characteristic has been overlooked, it is proper to point it out in a sentence or so. Do not compliment the board on the thoroughness of their examination – they have been sketchy, and you know it. If you wish, merely say, "No thank you, I have nothing further to add." This is a point where you can "talk yourself out" of a good impression or fail to present an important bit of information. Remember, *you close the interview yourself.*

The chairman will then say, "That is all, Mr. _______, thank you." Do not be startled; the interview is over, and quicker than you think. Thank him, gather your belongings and take your leave. Save your sigh of relief for the other side of the door.

How to put your best foot forward

Throughout this entire process, you may feel that the board individually and collectively is trying to pierce your defenses, seek out your hidden weaknesses and embarrass and confuse you. Actually, this is not true. They are obliged to make an appraisal of your qualifications for the job you are seeking, and they want to see you in your best light. Remember, they must interview all candidates and a non-cooperative candidate may become a failure in spite of their best efforts to bring out his qualifications. Here are 15 suggestions that will help you:

1) Be natural – Keep your attitude confident, not cocky

If you are not confident that you can do the job, do not expect the board to be. Do not apologize for your weaknesses, try to bring out your strong points. The board is interested in a positive, not negative, presentation. Cockiness will antagonize any board member and make him wonder if you are covering up a weakness by a false show of strength.

2) Get comfortable, but don't lounge or sprawl

Sit erectly but not stiffly. A careless posture may lead the board to conclude that you are careless in other things, or at least that you are not impressed by the importance of the occasion. Either conclusion is natural, even if incorrect. Do not fuss with your clothing, a pencil or an ashtray. Your hands may occasionally be useful to emphasize a point; do not let them become a point of distraction.

3) Do not wisecrack or make small talk

This is a serious situation, and your attitude should show that you consider it as such. Further, the time of the board is limited – they do not want to waste it, and neither should you.

4) Do not exaggerate your experience or abilities

In the first place, from information in the application or other interviews and sources, the board may know more about you than you think. Secondly, you probably will not get away with it. An experienced board is rather adept at spotting such a situation, so do not take the chance.

5) If you know a board member, do not make a point of it, yet do not hide it

Certainly you are not fooling him, and probably not the other members of the board. Do not try to take advantage of your acquaintanceship – it will probably do you little good.

6) Do not dominate the interview

Let the board do that. They will give you the clues – do not assume that you have to do all the talking. Realize that the board has a number of questions to ask you, and do not try to take up all the interview time by showing off your extensive knowledge of the answer to the first one.

7) Be attentive

You only have 20 minutes or so, and you should keep your attention at its sharpest throughout. When a member is addressing a problem or question to you, give him your undivided attention. Address your reply principally to him, but do not exclude the other board members.

8) Do not interrupt

A board member may be stating a problem for you to analyze. He will ask you a question when the time comes. Let him state the problem, and wait for the question.

9) Make sure you understand the question

Do not try to answer until you are sure what the question is. If it is not clear, restate it in your own words or ask the board member to clarify it for you. However, do not haggle about minor elements.

10) Reply promptly but not hastily

A common entry on oral board rating sheets is "candidate responded readily," or "candidate hesitated in replies." Respond as promptly and quickly as you can, but do not jump to a hasty, ill-considered answer.

11) Do not be peremptory in your answers

A brief answer is proper – but do not fire your answer back. That is a losing game from your point of view. The board member can probably ask questions much faster than you can answer them.

12) Do not try to create the answer you think the board member wants

He is interested in what kind of mind you have and how it works – not in playing games. Furthermore, he can usually spot this practice and will actually grade you down on it.

13) Do not switch sides in your reply merely to agree with a board member

Frequently, a member will take a contrary position merely to draw you out and to see if you are willing and able to defend your point of view. Do not start a debate, yet do not surrender a good position. If a position is worth taking, it is worth defending.

14) Do not be afraid to admit an error in judgment if you are shown to be wrong

The board knows that you are forced to reply without any opportunity for careful consideration. Your answer may be demonstrably wrong. If so, admit it and get on with the interview.

15) Do not dwell at length on your present job

The opening question may relate to your present assignment. Answer the question but do not go into an extended discussion. You are being examined for a *new* job, not your present one. As a matter of fact, try to phrase ALL your answers in terms of the job for which you are being examined.

Basis of Rating

Probably you will forget most of these "do's" and "don'ts" when you walk into the oral interview room. Even remembering them all will not ensure you a passing grade. Perhaps you did not have the qualifications in the first place. But remembering them will help you to put your best foot forward, without treading on the toes of the board members.

Rumor and popular opinion to the contrary notwithstanding, an oral board wants you to make the best appearance possible. They know you are under pressure – but they also want to see how you respond to it as a guide to what your reaction would be under the pressures of the job you seek. They will be influenced by the degree of poise you display, the personal traits you show and the manner in which you respond.

ABOUT THIS BOOK

This book contains tests divided into Examination Sections. Go through each test, answering every question in the margin. We have also attached a sample answer sheet at the back of the book that can be removed and used. At the end of each test look at the answer key and check your answers. On the ones you got wrong, look at the right answer choice and learn. Do not fill in the answers first. Do not memorize the questions and answers, but understand the answer and principles involved. On your test, the questions will likely be different from the samples. Questions are changed and new ones added. If you understand these past questions you should have success with any changes that arise. Tests may consist of several types of questions. We have additional books on each subject should more study be advisable or necessary for you. Finally, the more you study, the better prepared you will be. This book is intended to be the last thing you study before you walk into the examination room. Prior study of relevant texts is also recommended. NLC publishes some of these in our Fundamental Series. Knowledge and good sense are important factors in passing your exam. Good luck also helps. So now study this Passbook, absorb the material contained within and take that knowledge into the examination. Then do your best to pass that exam.

EXAMINATION SECTION

EXAMINATION SECTION
TEST 1

DIRECTIONS: Each question or incomplete statement is followed by several suggested answers or completions. Select the one that BEST answers the question or completes the statement. *PRINT THE LETTER OF THE CORRECT ANSWER IN THE SPACE AT THE RIGHT.*

Questions 1-10.

WORD MEANING

DIRECTIONS: Each question from 1 to 10 contains a word in capitals followed by four suggested meanings of the word. For each question, choose the best meaning. *PRINT THE LETTER OF THE CORRECT ANSWER IN THE SPACE AT THE RIGHT.*

1. ACCURATE 1.____
   A. correct B. useful C. afraid D. careless

2. ALTER 2.____
   A. copy B. change C. report D. agree

3. DOCUMENT 3.____
   A. outline B. agreement C. blueprint D. record

4. INDICATE 4.____
   A. listen B. show C. guess D. try

5. INVENTORY 5.____
   A. custom B. discovery C. warning D. list

6. ISSUE 6.____
   A. annoy B. use up C. give out D. gain

7. NOTIFY 7.____
   A. inform B. promise C. approve D. strengthen

8. ROUTINE 8.____
   A. path B. mistake C. habit D. journey

9. TERMINATE 9.____
   A. rest B. start C. deny D. end

10. TRANSMIT 10.____
    A. put in B. send C. stop D. go across

Questions 11-15.

READING COMPREHENSION

DIRECTIONS: Questions 11 through 15 test how well you understand what you read. It will be necessary for you to read carefully because your answers to these questions should be based ONLY on the information given in the following paragraphs.

The recipient gains an impression of a typewritten letter before he begins to read the message. Pastors which provide for a good first impression include margins and spacing that are visually pleasing, formal parts of the letter which are correctly placed according to the style of the letter, copy which is free of obvious erasures and over-strikes, and transcript that is even and clear. The problem for the typist is that of how to produce that first, positive impression of her work.

There are several general rules which a typist can follow when she wishes to prepare a properly spaced letter on a sheet of letter-head. Ordinarily, the width of a letter should not be less than four inches nor more than six inches. The side margins should also have a desirable relation to the bottom margin and the space between the letterhead and the body of the letter. Usually the most appealing arrangement is when the side margins are even and the bottom margin is slightly wider than the side margins. In some offices, however, standard line length is used for all business letters, and the secretary then varies the spacing between the date line and the inside address according to the length of the letter.

11. The BEST title for the above paragraphs would be: 11.____

    A. Writing Office Letters
    B. Making Good First Impressions
    C. Judging Well-Typed Letters
    D. Good Placing and Spacing for Office Letters

12. According to the above paragraphs, which of the following might be considered the way in which people very quickly judge the quality of work which has been typed? By 12.____

    A. measuring the margins to see if they are correct
    B. looking at the spacing and cleanliness of the typescript
    C. scanning the body of the letter for meaning
    D. reading the date line and address for errors

13. What, according to the above paragraphs, would be definitely UNDESIRABLE as the average line length of a typed letter? 13.____

    A. 4" B. 5" C. 6" D. 7"

14. According to the above paragraphs, when the line length is kept standard, the secretary 14.____

    A. does not have to vary the spacing at all since this also is standard
    B. adjusts the spacing between the date line and inside address for different lengths of letters
    C. uses the longest line as a guideline for spacing between the date line and inside address
    D. varies the number of spaces between the lines

15. According to the above paragraphs, side margins are MOST pleasing when they 15.____

A. are even and somewhat smaller than the bottom margin
B. are slightly wider than the bottom margin
C. vary with the length of the letter
D. are figured independently from the letterhead and the body of the letter

Questions 16-20.

CODING

DIRECTIONS:

Name of Applicant	H	A	N	G	S	B	R	U	K	E
Test Code	c	o	m	p	l	e	x	i	t	y
File Number	0	1	2	3	4	5	6	7	8	9

Assume that each of the above capital letters is the first letter of the name of an Applicant, that the small letter directly beneath each capital letter is the test code for the Applicant, and that the number directly beneath each code letter is the file number for the Applicant.

In each of the following Questions 16 through 20, the test code letters and the file numbers in Columns 2 and 3 should correspond to the capital letters in Column 1. For each question, look at each column carefully and mark your answer as follows:

If there is an error only in Column 2, mark your answer A.
If there is an error only in Column 3, mark your answer B.
If there is an error in both Columns 2 and 3, mark your answer C.
If both Columns 2 and 3 are correct, mark your answer D.

The following sample question is given to help you understand the procedure.

SAMPLE QUESTION

Column 1	Column 2	Column 3
AKEHN	otyci	18902

In Column 2, the final test code letter *i.* should be *m.* Column 3 is correctly coded to Column 1. Since there is an error only in Column 2, the answer is A.

	Column 1	Column 2	Column 3	
16.	NEKKU	mytti	29987	16.____
17.	KRAEB	txyle	86095	17.____
18.	ENAUK	ymoit	92178	18.____
19.	REANA	xeomo	69121	19.____
20.	EKHSE	ytcxy	97049	20.____

Questions 21-30.

ARITHMETICAL REASONING

21. If a secretary answered 28 phone calls and typed the addresses for 112 credit statements in one morning, what is the ratio of phone calls answered to credit statements typed for that period of time? 21.____

A. 1:4 B. 1:7 C. 2:3 D. 3:5

22. According to a suggested filing system, no more than 10 folders should be filed behind any one file guide and from 15 to 25 file guides should be used in each file drawer for easy finding and filing. 22.____
The maximum number of folders that a five-drawer file cabinet can hold to allow easy finding and filing is

A. 550 B. 750 C. 1,100 D. 1,250

23. An employee had a starting salary of $25,804. He received a salary increase at the end of each year, and at the end of the seventh year his salary was $33,476. 23.____
What was his average annual increase in salary over these seven years?

A. $1,020 B. $1,076 C. $1,096 D. $1,144

24. The 55 typists and 28 senior clerks in a certain city agency were paid a total of $1,943,200 in salaries last year. 24.____
If the average annual salary of a typist was $22,400 the average annual salary of a senior clerk was

A. $25,400 B. $26,600 C. $26,800 D. $27,000

25. A typist has been given a three page report to type. She has finished typing the first two pages. The first page has 283 words, and the second page has 366 words. 25.____
If the total report consists of 954 words, how many words will she have to type on the third page of the report?

A. 202 B. 287 C. 305 D. 313

26. In one day, Clerk A processed 30% more forms than Clerk B, and Clerk C processed li times as many forms as Clerk A. If Clerk B processed 40 forms, how many more forms were processed by Clerk C than Clerk B? 26.____

A. 12 B. 13 C. 21 D. 25

27. A clerk who earns a gross salary of $452 every two weeks has the following deductions taken from her paycheck: 27.____
15% for City, State, Federal taxes; 2 1/2% for Social Security; $1.30 for health insurance; and $6.00 for union dues. The amount of her take-home pay is

A. $256.20 B. $312.40 C. $331.60 D. $365.60

28. In 2005, a city agency spent $2,000 to buy pencils at a cost of $5.00 a dozen. 28.____
If the agency used 3/4 of these pencils in 2005 and used the same number of pencils in 2006, how many more pencils did it have to buy to have enough pencils for all of 2006?

A. 1,200 B. 2,400 C. 3,600 D. 4,800

29. A clerk who worked in Agency X earned the following salaries: $20,140 the first year,$21,000 the second year, and $21,920 the third year. Another clerk who worked in Agency Y for three years earned $21,100 a year for two years and $21,448 the third year. The difference between the average salaries received by both clerks over a three-year period is 29.____

A. $196 B. $204 C. $348 D. $564

30. An employee who works over 40 hours in any week receives overtime payment for the extra hours at time and one-half (1 1/2 times) his hourly rate of pay. An employee who earns $13.60 an hour works a total of 45 hours during a certain week.
His total pay for that week would be 30.____

A. $564.40 B. $612.00 C. $646.00 D. $812.00

Questions 31-35.

RELATED INFORMATION

31. To tell a newly-employed clerk to fill a top drawer of a four-drawer cabinet with heavy folders which will be often used and to keep lower drawers only partly filled is 31.____

A. *good,* because a tall person would have to bend unnecessarily if he had to use a lower drawer
B. *bad,* because the file cabinet may tip over when the top drawer is opened
C. *good,* because it is the most easily reachable drawer for the average person
D. *bad,* because a person bending down at another drawer may accidentally bang his head on the bottom of the drawer when he straightens up

32. If a senior typist or senior clerk has requisitioned a *ream* of paper in order to duplicate a single page office announcement, how many announcements can be printed from the one package of paper? 32.____

A. 200 B. 500 C. 700 D. 1,000

33. Your supervisor has asked you to locate a telephone number for an attorney named Jones, whose office is located at 311 Broadway, and whose name is not already listed in your files.
The BEST method for finding the number would be for you to 33.____

A. call the information operator and have her get it for you
B. look in the alphabetical directory (white pages) under the name Jones at 311 Broadway
C. refer to the heading Attorney in the yellow pages for the name Jones at 311 Broadway
D. ask your supervisor who referred her to Mr. Jones, then call that person for the number

34. An example of material that should NOT be sent by first class mail is a 34.____

A. email copy of a letter
B. post card
C. business reply card
D. large catalogue

35. In the operations of a government agency, a voucher is ORDINARILY used to 35.____

A. refer someone to the agency for a position or assignment
B. certify that an agency's records of financial trans-actions are accurate
C. order payment from agency funds of a stated amount to an individual
D. enter a statement of official opinion in the records of the agency

Questions 36-40.

ENGLISH USAGE

DIRECTIONS: Each question from 36 through 40 contains a sentence. Read each sentence carefully to decide whether it is correct. Then, in the space at the right, mark your answer:

(A) if the sentence is incorrect because of bad grammar or sentence structure

(B) if the sentence is incorrect because of bad punctuation

(C) if the sentence is incorrect because of bad capitalization

(D) if the sentence is correct

Each incorrect sentence has only one type of error. Consider a sentence correct if it has no errors, although there may be other correct ways of saying the same thing.

SAMPLE QUESTION I: One of our clerks were promoted yesterday.

The subject of this sentence is *one,* so the verb should be *was promoted* instead of *were promoted.* Since the sentence is incorrect because of bad grammar, the answer to Sample Question I is (A).

SAMPLE QUESTION II: Between you and me, I would prefer not going there.

Since this sentence is correct, the answer to Sample Question II is (D).

36. The National alliance of Businessmen is trying to persuade private businesses to hire youth in the summertime. 36.____

37. The supervisor who is on vacation, is in charge of processing vouchers. 37.____

38. The activity of the committee at its conferences is always stimulating. 38.____

39. After checking the addresses again, the letters went to the mailroom. 39.____

40. The director, as well as the employees, are interested in sharing the dividends. 40.____

Questions 41-45.

FILING

DIRECTIONS: Each question from 41 through 45 contains four names. For each question, choose the name that should be FIRST if the four names are to be arranged in alphabeti-cal order in accordance with the Rules for Alphabetical Filing given below. Read these rules carefully. Then, for each question, indicate in the space at the right the letter before the name that should be FIRST in alphabet-ical order.

RULES FOR ALPHABETICAL FILING

Names of People

(1) The names of people are filed in strict alphabetical order, first according to the last name, then according to first name or initial, and finally according to middle name or initial. FOR EXAMPLE: George Allen comes before Edward Bell, and Leonard P. Reston comes before Lucille B. Reston.

(2) When last names are the same, FOR EXAMPLE, A. Green and Agnes Green, the one with the initial comes before the one with the name written out when the first initials are identi-cal.

(3) When first and last names are alike and the middle name is given, FOR EXAMPLE, John David Doe and John Devoe Doe, the names should be filed in the alphabetical order of the middle names.

(4) When first and last names are the same, a name without a middle initial comes before one with a middle name or initial. FOR EXAMPLE, John Doe comes before both John A. Doe and John Alan Doe.

(5) When first and last names are the same, a name with a middle initial comes before one with a middle name beginning with the same initial. FOR EXAMPLE: Jack R. Hertz comes before Jack Richard Hertz.

(6) Prefixes such as De, O', Mac, Mc, and Van are filed as written and are treated as part of the names to which they are connected. FOR EXAMPLE: Robert O'Dea is filed before David Olsen.

(7) Abbreviated names are treated as if they were spelled out. FOR EXAMPLE: Chas. is filed as Charles and Thos. is filed as Thomas.

(8) Titles and designations such as Dr., Mr., and Prof, are disregarded in filing.

Names of Organizations

(1) The names of business organizations are filed according to the order in which each word in the name appears. When an organization name bears the name of a person, it is filed according to the rules for filing names of people as given above. FOR EXAMPLE: William Smith Service Co. comes before Television Distributors, Inc.

(2) *Where bureau, board, office, or department appears as the first part of the title of a governmental agency, that agency should be filed under the word in the title expressing the chief function of the agency. FOR EXAMPLE: Bureau of the Budget would be filed as if written Budget, (Bureau of the). The Department of Personnel would be filed as if written Personnel, (Department of).*

(3) *When the following words are part of an organization, they are disregarded: the, of, and.*

(4) *When there are numbers in a name, they are treated as if they were spelled out. FOR EXAMPLE: 10th Street Bootery is filed as Tenth Street Bootery.*

<u>SAMPLE QUESTION:</u>

A. Jane Earl (2)
B. James A. Earle (4)
C. James Earl (1)
D. J. Earle (3)

The numbers in parentheses show the proper alphabetical order in which these names should be filed. Since the name that should be filed FIRST is James Earl, the answer to the Sample Question is (C).

41. A. Majorca Leather Goods
B. Robert Maiorca and Sons
C. Maintenance Management Corp.
D. Majestic Carpet Mills
41.____

42. A. Municipal Telephone Service
B. Municipal Reference Library
C. Municipal Credit Union
D. Municipal Broadcasting System
42.____

43. A. Robert B. Pierce B. R. Bruce Pierce
C. Ronald Pierce D. Robert Bruce Pierce
43.____

44. A. Four Seasons Sports Club B. 14th. St. Shopping Center
C. Forty Thieves Restaurant D. 42nd St. Theaters
44.____

45. A. Franco Franceschini B. Amos Franchini
C. Sandra Franceschia D. Lilie Franchinesca
45.____

Questions 46-50.

SPELLING

DIRECTIONS: In each question, one of the words is misspelled. Select the letter of the misspelled word. *PRINT THE LETTER OF THE CORRECT ANSWER IN THE SPACE AT THE RIGHT.*

46. A. option B. extradite
C. comparitive D. jealousy
46.____

47. A. handicaped B. assurance
C. sympathy D. speech
47.____

48.	A. recommend C. disapprove	B. carraige D. independent	48.____
49.	A. ingenuity C. uncanny	B. tenet (opinion) D. intrigueing	49.____
50.	A. arduous C. iervant	B. hideous D. companies	50.____

KEY (CORRECT ANSWERS)

1.	A	11.	D	21.	A	31.	B	41.	C
2.	B	12.	B	22.	D	32.	B	42.	D
3.	D	13.	D	23.	C	33.	C	43.	B
4.	B	14.	B	24.	A	34.	D	44.	D
5.	D	15.	A	25.	C	35.	C	45.	C
6.	C	16.	B	26.	D	36.	C	46.	C
7.	A	17.	C	27.	D	37.	B	47.	A
8.	C	18.	D	28.	B	38.	D	48.	B
9.	D	19.	A	29.	A	39.	A	49.	D
10.	B	20.	C	30.	C	40.	A	50.	C'

EXAMINATION SECTION

TEST 1

DIRECTIONS: Each question or incomplete statement is followed by several suggested answers or completions. Select the one that BEST answers the question or completes the statement. *PRINT THE LETTER OF THE CORRECT ANSWER IN THE SPACE AT THE RIGHT.*

Questions 1-5.

DIRECTIONS: Questions 1 through 5 consist of a sentence with an underlined word. For each question, select the choice that is CLOSEST in meaning to the underlined word.

EXAMPLE
This division reviews the fiscal reports of the agency.
In this sentence, the word *fiscal* means MOST NEARLY
A. financial B. critical C. basic D. personnel
The correct answer is A. "financial" because "financial" is closest to *fiscal*.
Therefore, the answer is A.

1. Every good office worker needs basic skills. 1.____
The word *basic* in this sentence means
A. fundamental B. advanced C. unusual D. outstanding

2. He turned out to be a good instructor. 2.____
The word *instructor* in this sentence means
A. student B. worker C. typist D. teacher

3. The quantity of work in the office was under study. 3.____
In this sentence, the word *quantity* means
A. amount B. flow C. supervision D. type

4. The morning was spent examining the time records. 4.____
In this sentence, the word *examining* means
A. distributing B. collecting C. checking D. filing

5. The candidate filled in the proper spaces on the form. 5.____
In this sentence, the word *proper* means
A. blank B. appropriate C. many D. remaining

Questions 6-8.

DIRECTIONS: Questions 6 through 8 are to be answered SOLELY on the basis of the information contained in the following paragraph.

The increase in the number of public documents in the last two centuries closely matches the increase in population in the United States. The great number of public documents has become a serious threat to their usefulness. It is necessary to have programs which will reduce the number of public documents that are kept and which will, at the same time, assure keeping those that have value. Such programs need a great deal of thought to have any success.

6. According to the above paragraph, public documents may be less useful if 6.____
   A. the files are open to the public
   B. the record room is too small
   C. the copying machine is operated only during normal working hours
   D. too many records are being kept

7. According to the above paragraph, the growth of the population in the United States has matched the growth in the quantity of public documents for a period of MOST NEARLY _____ years. 7.____
   A. 50 B. 100 C. 200 D. 300

8. According to the above paragraph, the increased number of public documents has made it necessary to 8.____
   A. find out which public documents are worth keeping
   B. reduce the great number of public documents by decreasing government services
   C. eliminate the copying of all original public documents
   D. avoid all new copying devices

Questions 9-10.

DIRECTIONS: Questions 9 and 10 are to be answered SOLELY on the basis of the information contained in the following paragraph.

The work goals of an agency can best be reached if the employees understand and agree with these goals. One way to gain such understanding and agreement is for management to encourage and seriously consider suggestions from employees in the setting of agency goals.

9. On the basis of the above paragraph, the BEST way to achieve the work goals of an agency is to 9.____
   A. make certain that employees work as hard as possible
   B. study the organizational structure of the agency
   C. encourage employees to think seriously about the agency's problems
   D. stimulate employee understanding of the work goals

10. On the basis of the above paragraph, understanding and agreement with agency goals can be gained by 10.____
   A. allowing the employees to set agency goals
   B. reaching agency goals quickly
   C. legislative review of agency operations
   D. employee participation in setting agency goals

Questions 11-15.

DIRECTIONS: Each of Questions 11 through 15 consists of a group of four words. One word in each group is incorrectly spelled. For each question, print the letter of the correct answer in the space at the right that is the same as the letter next to the word which is INCORRECTLY spelled.

EXAMPLE

A. housing B. certain C. budgit D. money

The word "budgit" is incorrectly spelled, because the correct spelling should be "budget." Therefore, the correct answer is C.

11. A. sentince B. bulletin C. notice D. definition 11.____

12. A. appointment B. exactly C. typest D. light 12.____

13. A. penalty B. suparvise C. consider D. division 13.____

14. A. schedule B. accurate C. corect D. simple 14.____

15. A. suggestion B. installed C. proper D. agincy 15.____

Questions 16-20.

DIRECTIONS: Each Question 16 through 20 consists of a sentence which may be
   A. incorrect because of bad word usage, or
   B. incorrect because of bad punctuation, or
   C. incorrect because of bad spelling, or
   D. correct

Read each sentence carefully. Then print in the space at the right A, B, C, or D, according to the answer you choose from the four choices listed above. There is only one type of error in each incorrect sentence. If there is no error, the sentence is correct.

EXAMPLE

George Washington was the father of his contry.
This sentence is incorrect because of bad spelling ("contry" instead of "country"). Therefore, the answer is C.

16. The assignment was completed in record time but the payroll for it has not yet been preparid. 16.____

17. The operator, on the other hand, is willing to learn me how to use the mimeograph. 17.____

18. She is the prettiest of the three sisters. 18.____

19. She doesn't know; if the mail has arrived. 19.____

20. The doorknob of the office door is broke. 20.____

21. A clerk can process a form in 15 minutes. 21.____
How many forms can that clerk process in six hours?
A. 10 B. 21 C. 24 D. 90

22. An office staff consists of 120 people. Sixty of them have been assigned to a special project. Of the remaining staff, 20 answer the mail, 10 handle phone calls, and the rest operate the office machines. 22.____
The number of people operating the office machines is
A. 20 B. 30 C. 40 D. 45

23. An office worker received 65 applications but on the first day had to return 26 of them for being incomplete and on the second day 25 had to be returned for being incomplete. 23.____
How many applications did NOT have to be returned?
A. 10 B. 12 C. 14 D. 16

24. An office worker answered 63 phone calls in one day and 91 phone calls the next day. 24.____
For these 2 days, what was the average number of phone calls he answered per day?
A. 77 B. 28 C. 82 D. 93

25. An office worker processed 12 vouchers of $8.50 each, 3 vouchers of $3.68 each, and 2 vouchers of $1.29 each. 25.____
The TOTAL dollar amount of these vouchers is
A. $116.04 B. $117.52 C. $118.62 D. $119.04

KEY (CORRECT ANSWERS)

1. A
2. D
3. A
4. C
5. B

6. D
7. C
8. A
9. D
10. D

11. A
12. C
13. B
14. C
15. D

16. C
17. A
18. D
19. B
20. A

21. C
22. B
23. C
24. A
25. C

TEST 2

DIRECTIONS: Each question or incomplete statement is followed by several suggested answers or completions. Select the one that BEST answers the question or completes the statement. *PRINT THE LETTER OF THE CORRECT ANSWER IN THE SPACE AT THE RIGHT.*

Questions 1-5.

DIRECTIONS: Each Question from 1 through 5 lists four names. The names may not be exactly the same. Compare the names in each question and mark your answer

A if all the names are different
B if only two names are exactly the same
C if only three names are exactly the same
D if all four names are exactly the same

EXAMPLE
Jensen, Alfred E.
Jensen, Alfred E.
Jensan, Alfred E.
Jensen, Fred E.

Since the name Jensen, Alfred E. appears twice and is exactly the same in both places, the correct answer is B.

1. A. Riviera, Pedro S. B. Rivers, Pedro S. 1.____
C. Riviera, Pedro N. D. Riviera, Juan S.

2. A. Guider, Albert B. Guidar, Albert 2.____
C. Giuder, Alfred D. Guider, Albert

3. A. Blum, Rona B. Blum, Rona 3.____
C. Blum, Rona D. Blum, Rona

4. A. Raugh, John B. Raugh, James 4.____
C. Raughe, John D. Raugh, John

5. A. Katz, Stanley B. Katz, Stanley 5.____
C. Katze, Stanley D. Katz, Stanley

Questions 6-10.

DIRECTIONS: Each Question 6 through 10 consists of numbers or letters in Columns I and II. For each question, compare each line of Column I with its corresponding line in Column II and decide how many lines in Column I are EXACTLY the same as their corresponding lines in Column II. In your answer space, mark your answer

A if only ONE line in Column I is exactly the same as its corresponding line in Column II
B if only TWO lines in Column I are exactly the same as their corresponding lines in Column II

C if only THREE lines in Column I are exactly the same as their corresponding lines in Column II
D if all FOUR lines in Column I are exactly the same as their corresponding lines in Column II

EXAMPLE

Column I	Column II
1776	1776
1865	1865
1945	1945
1976	1978

Only three lines in Column I are exactly the same as their corresponding lines in Column II. Therefore, the correct answer is C.

	Column I	Column II	
6.	5653	5653	6.____
	8727	8728	
	ZPSS	ZPSS	
	4952	9453	
7.	PNJP	PNPJ	7.____
	NJPJ	NJPJ	
	JNPN	JNPN	
	PNJP	PNPJ	
8.	effe	eFfe	8.____
	uWvw	uWvw	
	KpGj	KpGg	
	vmnv	vmnv	
9.	5232	5232	9.____
	PfrC	PfrN	
	zssz	zzss	
	rwwr	rwww	
10.	czws	czws	10.____
	cecc	cece	
	thrm	thrm	
	lwtz	lwtz	

Questions 11-15.

DIRECTIONS: Questions 11 through 15 have lines of letters and numbers. Each letter should be matched with its number in accordance with the following table.

Letter	F	R	C	A	W	L	E	N	B	T
Matching Number	0	1	2	3	4	5	6	7	8	9

From the table you can determine that the letter F has the matching number 0 below it, the letter R has the matching number 1 below, etc.
For each question, compare each line of letters and numbers carefully to see if each letter has its correct matching number. If all the letters and numbers are matched correctly in
none of the lines of the question, mark your answer A
only *one* of the lines of the question, mark your answer B
only *two* of the lines of the question, mark your answer C
all three lines of the question, mark your answer D

EXAMPLE

WBCR	4826
TLBF	9580
ATNE	3986

There is a mistake in the first line because the letter R should have its matching number 1 instead of the number 6.

The second line is correct because each letter shown has the correct matching number.

There is a mistake in the third line because the letter N should have the matching number 7 instead of the number 8.

Since all the letters and numbers are correct matched in only one of the lines in the sample, the correct answer is B.

11. EBCT 6829 — 11.____
ATWR 3961
NLBW 7584

12. RNCT 1729 — 12.____
LNCR 5728
WAEB 5368

13. NTWB 7948 — 13.____
RABL 1385
TAEF 9360

14. LWRB 5417 — 14.____
RLWN 1647
CBWA 2843

15. ABTC 3792 — 15.____
WCER 5261
AWCN 3417

16. Your job often brings you into contact with the public. 16.____
Of the following, it would be MOST desirable to explain the reasons for official actions to people coming into your office for assistance because such explanations
A. help build greater understanding between the public and your agency
B. help build greater self-confidence in city employees
C. convince the public that nothing they do can upset a city employee
D. show the public that city employees are intelligent

17. Assume that you strongly dislike one of your co-workers. 17.____
You should FIRST
   A. discuss your feeling with the co-worker
   B. demand a transfer to another office
   C. suggest to your supervisor that the co-worker should be observed carefully
   D. try to figure out the reason for this dislike before you say or do anything

18. An office worker who has problems accepting authority is MOST likely to find it difficult to 18.____
   A. obey rules
   B. understand people
   C. assist other employees
   D. follow complex instructions

19. The employees in your office have taken a dislike to one person and frequently annoy her. 19.____
Your supervisor should
   A. transfer this person to another unit at the first opportunity
   B. try to find out the reason for the staff's attitude before doing anything about it
   C. threaten to transfer the first person observed bothering this person
   D. ignore the situation

20. Assume that your supervisor has asked a worker in your office to get a copy of a report out of the files. You notice the worker as accidentally pulled out the wrong report. 20.____
Of the following, the BEST way for you to handle this situation is to tell
   A. the worker about all the difficulties that will result from this error
   B. the worker about her mistake in a nice way
   C. the worker to ignore this error
   D. your supervisor that this worker needs more training in how to use the files

21. Filing systems differ in their efficiency. 21.____
Which of the following is the BEST way to evaluate the efficiency of a filing system? A
   A. number of times used per day
   B. amount of material that is received each day for filing
   C. amount of time it takes to locate material
   D. type of locking system used

22. In planning ahead so that a sufficient amount of general office supplies is always available, it would be LEAST important to find out the 22.____
   A. current office supply needs of the staff
   B. amount of office supplies used last year
   C. days and times that office supplies can be ordered
   D. agency goals and objectives

23. The MAIN reason for establishing routine office work procedures is that once a routine is established 23.____
    A. work need not be checked for accuracy
    B. all steps in the routine will take an equal amount of time to perform
    C. each time the job is repeated, it will take less time to perform
    D. each step in the routine will not have to be planned all over again each time

24. When an office machine centrally located in an agency must be shut down for repairs, the bureaus and divisions using this machine should be informed of the 24.____
    A. expected length of time before the machine will be in operation again
    B. estimated cost of repairs
    C. efforts being made to avoid future repairs
    D. type of new equipment which the agency may buy in the future to replace the machine being repaired

25. If the day's work is properly scheduled, the MOST important result would be that the 25.____
    A. supervisor will not have to do much supervision
    B. employee will know what to do next
    C. employee will show greater initiative
    D. job will become routine

KEY (CORRECT ANSWERS)

1.	A	11.	C
2.	B	12.	B
3.	D	13.	D
4.	B	14.	B
5.	C	15.	A
6.	B	16.	A
7.	B	17.	D
8.	B	18.	A
9.	A	19.	B
10.	C	20.	B

21.	C
22.	D
23.	D
24.	A
25.	B

CLERICAL ABILITIES TEST

EXAMINATION SECTION

TEST 1

DIRECTIONS: Each question or incomplete statement is followed by several suggested answers or completions. Select the one that BEST answers the question or completes the statement. *PRINT THE LETTER OF THE CORRECT ANSWER IN THE SPACE AT THE RIGHT.*

Questions 1-10.

DIRECTIONS: Questions 1 through 10 consist of lines of names, dates, and numbers. For each question, you are to choose the option (A, B, C, or D) in Column II which EXACTLY matches the information in Column I. *PRINT THE LETTER OF THE CORRECT ANSWER IN THE SPACE AT THE RIGHT.*

SAMPLE QUESTION

Column I	Column II
Schneider 11/16/75 581932	A. Schneider 11/16/75 518932
	B. Schneider 11/16/75 581932
	C. Schnieder 11/16/75 581932
	D. Shnieder 11/16/75 518932

The correct answer is B. Only Option B shows the name, date, and number exactly as they are in Column I. Option A has a mistake in the number. Option C has a mistake in the name. Option D has a mistake in the name and in the number. Now answer Questions 1 through 10 in the same manner.

	Column I	Column II	
1.	Johnston 12/26/74 659251	A. Johnson 12/23/74 659251	1.____
		B. Johston 12/26/74 659251	
		C. Johnston 12/26/74 695251	
		D. Johnston 12/26/74 659251	
2.	Allison 1/26/75 9939256	A. Allison 1/26/75 9939256	2.____
		B. Alisson 1/26/75 9939256	
		C. Allison 1/26/76 9399256	
		D. Allison 1/26/75 9993356	
3.	Farrell 2/12/75 361251	A. Farell 2/21/75 361251	3.____
		B. Farrell 2/12/75 361251	
		C. Farrell 2/21/75 361251	
		D. Farrell 2/12/75 361151	

4. Guerrero 4/28/72 105689
A. Guererro 4/28/72 105689
B. Guererro 4/28/72 105986
C. Guerrero 4/28/72 105869
D. Guerrero 4/28/72 105689
4.____

5. McDonnell 6/05/73 478215
A. McDonnell 6/15/73 478215
B. McDonnell 6/05/73 478215
C. McDonnell 6/05/73 472815
D. MacDonell 6/05/73 478215
5.____

6. Shepard 3/31/71 075421
A. Sheperd 3/31/71 075421
B. Shepard 3/13/71 075421
C. Shepard 3/31/71 075421
D. Shepard 3/13/71 075241
6.____

7. Russell 4/01/69 031429
A. Russell 4/01/69 031429
B. Russell 4/10/69 034129
C. Russell 4/10/69 031429
D. Russell 4/01/69 034129
7.____

8. Phillips 10/16/68 961042
A. Philipps 10/16/68 961042
B. Phillips 10/16/68 960142
C. Phillips 10/16/68 961042
D. Philipps 10/16/68 916042
8.____

9. Campbell 11/21/72 624856
A. Campbell 11/21/72 624856
B. Campbell 11/21/72 624586
C. Campbell 11/21/72 624686
D. Campbel 11/21/72 624856
9.____

10. Patterson 9/18/71 76199176
A. Patterson 9/18/72 76191976
B. Patterson 9/18/71 76199176
C. Patterson 9/18/72 76199176
D. Patterson 9/18/71 76919176
10.____

Questions 11-15.

DIRECTIONS: Questions 11 through 15 consist of groups of numbers and letters which you are to compare. For each question, you are to choose the option (A, B,C, or D) in Column I which EXACTLY matches the group of numbers and letters given in Column I.

SAMPLE QUESTION

<u>Column I</u>
B92466

<u>Column II</u>
A. B92644
B. B94266
C. A92466
D. B92466

The correct answer is D. Only Option D in Column II shows the group of numbers and letters EXACTLY as it appears in Column I. Now answer Questions 11 through 15 in the same manner.

	Column I	Column II	
11.	925AC5	A. 952CA5 B. 925AC5 C. 952AC5 D. 925CA6	11.____
12.	Y006925	A. Y060925 B. Y006295 C. Y006529 D. Y006925	12.____
13.	J236956	A. J236956 B. J326965 C. J239656 D. J932656	13.____
14.	AB6952	A. AB6952 B. AB9625 C. AB9652 D. AB6925	14.____
15.	X259361	A. X529361 B. X259631 C. X523961 D. X259361	15.____

Questions 16-25.

DIRECTIONS: Each of questions 16 through 25 consists of three lines of code letters and three lines of numbers. The numbers on each line should correspond with the code letters on the same line in accordance with the table below.

Code Letter	S	V	W	A	Q	M	X	E	G	K
Corresponding Number	0	1	2	3	4	5	5	7	8	9

On some of the lines, an error exists in the coding. Compare the letters and numbers in each question carefully. If you find an error or errors on:

only one of the lines in the question, mark your answer A;
any two lines in the question, mark your answer B;
all three lines in the question, mark your answer C;
none of the lines in the question, mark your answer D.

SAMPLE QUESTION

WQGKSXG	2489068
XEKVQMA	6591453
KMAESXV	9527061

In the above sample, the first line is correct since each code letter listed has the correct corresponding number. On the second line, an error exists because code letter E should have the number 7 instead of the number 5. On the third line, an error exists because the code letter A should have the number 3 instead of the number 2. Since there are errors in two of the three lines, the correct answer is B. Now answer Questions 16 through 25 in the same manner.

16. SWQEKGA 0247983
KEAVSXM 9731065
SSAXGKQ 0036894
16.____

17. QAMKMVS 4259510
MGGEASX 5897306
KSWMKWS 9125920
17.____

18. WKXQWVE 2964217
QKXXQVA 4966413
AWMXGVS 3253810
18.____

19. GMMKASE 8559307
AWVSKSW 3210902
QAVSVGK 4310189
19.____

20. XGKQSMK 6894049
QSVKEAS 4019730
GSMXKMV 8057951
20.____

21. AEKMWSG 3195208
MKQSVQK 5940149
XGQAEVW 6843712
21.____

22. XGMKAVS 6858310
SKMAWEQ 0953174
GVMEQSA 8167403
22.____

23. VQSKAVE 1489317
WQGKAEM 2489375
MEGKAWQ 5689324
23.____

24. XMQVSKG 6541098
QMEKEWS 4579720
KMEVGKG 9571983
24.____

25. GKVAMEW 88912572 25.____
AXMVKAE 3651937
KWAGMAV 9238531

Questions 26-35.

DIRECTIONS: Each of Questions 26 through 35 consists of a column of figures. For each question, add the column of figures and choose the correct answer from the four choices given.

26. 26.____
5,665.43
2,356.69
6,447.24
7,239.65

A. 20,698.01
B. 21,709.01
C. 21,718.01
D. 22,609.01

27. 27.____
817,209.55
264,354.29
82,368.76
849,964.89

A. 1,893.977.49
B. 1,989,988.39
C. 2,009,077.39
D. 2,013,897.49

28. 28.____
156,366.89
249,973.23
823,229.49
56,869.45

A. 1,286,439.06
B. 1,287,521.06
C. 1,297,539.06
D. 1,296,421.06

29. 29.____
23,422.15
149,696.24
238,377.53
86,289.79
505,533.63

A. 989,229.34
B. 999,879.34
C. 1,003,330.34
D. 1,023,329.34

30. 2,468,926.70
656,842.28
49,723.15
832,369.59 30.____

A. 3,218,062.72
B. 3,808,092.72
C. 4,007,861.72
D. 4,818,192.72

31. 524,201.52
7,775,678.51
8,345,299.63
40,628,898.08
31,374,670.07 31.____

A. 88,646,647.81
B. 88,646,747.91
C. 88,648,647.91
D. 88,648,747.81

32. 6,824,829.40
682,482.94
5,542,015.27
775,678.51
7,732,507.25 32.____

A. 21,557,513.37
B. 21,567,513.37
C. 22,567,503.37
D. 22,567,513.37

33. 22,109,405.58
6,097,093.43
5,050,073.99
8,118,050.05
4,313,980.82 33.____

A. 45,688,593.87
B. 45,688,603.87
C. 45,689,593.87
D. 45,689,603.87

34. 79,324,114.19
99,848,129.74
43,331,653.31
41,610,207.14 34.____

A. 264,114,104.38
B. 264,114,114.38
C. 265,114,114.38
D. 265,214,104.38

35. 33,729,653.94 35.____
5,959,342.58
26,052,715.47
4,452,669.52
7,079,953.59

A. 76,374,334.10
B. 76,375,334.10
C. 77,274,335.10
D. 77,275,335.10

Questions 36-40.

DIRECTIONS: Each of Questions 36 through 40 consists of a single number in Column I and four options in Column II. For each question, you are to choose the option (A, B, C, or D) in Column II which EXACTLY matches the number in Column I.

SAMPLE QUESTION

Column I	Column II
5965121	A. 5956121
	B. 5965121
	C. 5966121
	D. 5965211

The correct answer is B. Only Option B shows the number EXACTLY as it appears in Column I. Now answer Questions 36 through 40 in the same manner.

	Column I	Column II	
36.	9643242	A. 9643242	36.____
		B. 9462342	
		C. 9642442	
		D. 9463242	
37.	3572477	A. 3752477	37.____
		B. 3725477	
		C. 3572477	
		D. 3574277	
38.	5276101	A. 5267101	38.____
		B. 5726011	
		C. 5271601	
		D. 5276101	
39.	4469329	A. 4496329	39.____
		B. 4469329	
		C. 4496239	
		D. 4469239	

40. 2326308

A. 2236308
B. 2233608
C. 2326308
D. 2323608

40.____

KEY (CORRECT ANSWERS)

1.	D	11.	B	21.	A	31.	D
2.	A	12.	D	22.	C	32.	A
3.	B	13.	A	23.	B	33.	B
4.	D	14.	A	24.	D	34.	A
5.	B	15.	D	25.	A	35.	C
6.	C	16.	D	26.	B	36.	A
7.	A	17.	C	27.	D	37.	C
8.	C	18.	A	28.	A	38.	D
9.	A	19.	D	29.	C	39.	B
10.	B	20.	B	30.	C	40.	C

TEST 2

DIRECTIONS: Each question or incomplete statement is followed by several suggested answers or completions. Select the one that BEST answers the question or completes the statement. *PRINT THE LETTER OF THE CORRECT ANSWER IN THE SPACE AT THE RIGHT.*

Questions 1-5.

DIRECTIONS: Each of Questions 1 through 5 consists of a name and a dollar amount. In each question, the name and dollar amount in Column II should be an EXACT copy of the name and dollar amount in Column I. If there is:
a mistake only in the name, mark your answer A;
a mistake only in the dollar amount, mark your answer B;
a mistake in both the name and the dollar amount, mark your answer C;
no mistake in either the name or the dollar amount, mark your answer D.

SAMPLE QUESTION

Column I	Column II
George Peterson $125.50	George Petersson $125.50

Compare the name and dollar amount in Column II with the name and dollar amount in Column I. The name *Petersson* in Column II is spelled *Peterson* in Column I. The amount is the same in both columns. Since there is a mistake only in the name, the answer to the sample question is A. Now answer Questions 1 through 5 in the same manner.

	Column I	Column II	
1.	Susanne Shultz $3440	Susanne Schultz $3440	1.____
2.	Anibal P. Contrucci $2121.61	Anibel P. Contrucci $2112.61	2.____
3.	Eugenio Mendoza $12.45	Eugenio Mendozza $12.45	3.____
4.	Maurice Gluckstadt $4297	Maurice Gluckstadt $4297	4.____
5.	John Pampellonne $4656.94	John Pammpellonne $4566.94	5.____

Questions 6-11.

DIRECTIONS: Each of Questions 6 through 11 consist of a set of names and addresses, which you are to compare. In each question, the name and addresses in Column II should be an EXACT copy of the name and address in Column I. If there is:
a mistake only in the name, mark your answer A;
a mistake only in the address, mark your answer B;
a mistake in both the name and address, mark your answer C;
no mistake in either the name or address, mark your answer D.

SAMPLE QUESTION

Column I	Column II
Michael Filbert 456 Reade Street New York, N.Y. 10013	Michael Filbert 645 Reade Street New York, N.Y. 10013

Since there is a mistake only in the address (the street number should be 456 instead of 645), the answer to the sample question is B. Now answer Questions 6 through 11 in the same manner.

	Column I	Column II	
6.	Hilda Goettelmann 55 Lenox Rd. Brooklyn, N.Y. 11226	Hilda Goettelman 55 Lenox Ave. Brooklyn, N.Y. 11226	6.____
7.	Arthur Sherman 2522 Batchelder St. Brooklyn, N.Y. 11235	Arthur Sharman 2522 Batcheder St. Brooklyn, N.Y. 11253	7.____
8.	Ralph Barnett 300 West 28 Street New York, New York 10001	Ralph Barnett 300 West 28 Street New York, New York 10001	8.____
9.	George Goodwin 135 Palmer Avenue Staten Island, New York 10302	George Godwin 135 Palmer Avenue Staten Island, New York 10302	9.____
10.	Alonso Ramirez 232 West 79 Street New York, N.Y. 10024	Alonso Ramirez 223 West 79 Street New York, N.Y. 10024	10.____
11.	Cynthia Graham 149-34 83 Street Howard Beach, N.Y. 11414	Cynthia Graham 149-35 83 Street Howard Beach, N.Y. 11414	11.____

Questions 12-20.

DIRECTIONS: Questions 12 through 20 are problems in subtraction. For each question do the subtraction and select your answer from the four choices given.

12. 232,921.85
-179,587.68 12.____

A. 52,433.17 B. 52,434.17
C. 53,334.17 D. 53,343,17

13. 5,531,876.29
-3,897,158.36 13.____

A. 1,634,717.93 B. 1,644,718.93
C. 1,734,717.93 D. 1,7234,718.93

14. 1,482,658.22
-937,925.76 14.____

A. 544,633.46 B. 544,732.46
C. 545,632.46 D. 545,732.46

15. 937,828.17
-259,673.88 15.____

A. 678,154.29 B. 679,154.29
C. 688,155.39 D. 699,155.39

16. 760,412.38
-263,465.95 16.____

A. 496,046.43 B. 496,946.43
C. 496,956.43 D. 497,046.43

17. 3,203,902.26
-2,933,087.96 17.____

A. 260,814.30 B. 269,824.30
C. 270,814.30 D. 270,824.30

18. 1,023,468.71
-934,678.88 18.____

A. 88,780.83 B. 88,789.83
C. 88,880.83 D. 88,889.83

19. 831,549.47
-772,814.78 19.____

A. 58,734.69
B. 58,834.69
C. 59,735.69
D. 59,834.69

20. 6,306,181.74
-3,617,376.99 20.____

A. 2,687,904.99
B. 2,688,904.99
C. 2,689,804.99
D. 2,799,905.99

Questions 21-30.

DIRECTIONS: Each of Questions 21 through 30 consists of three lines of code letters and three lines of numbers. The numbers on each line should correspond with the code letters on the same line in accordance with the table below.

Code Letter	J	U	B	T	Y	D	K	R	L	P
Corresponding Number	0	1	2	3	4	5	5	7	8	9

On some of the lines, an error exists in the coding. Compare the letters and numbers in each question carefully. If you find an error or errors on:
only *one* of the lines in the question, mark your answer A;
any *two* lines in the question, mark your answer B;
all *three* lines in the question, mark your answer C;
none of the lines in the question, mark your answer D.

SAMPLE QUESTION

BJRPYUR	2079417
DTBPYKJ	5328460
YKLDBLT	4685283

In the above sample, the first line is correct since each code letter listed has the correct corresponding number. On the second line, an error exists because code letter P should have the number 9 instead of the number 8. The third line is correct since each code letter listed has the correct corresponding number. Since there is an error in *one* of the three lines, the correct answer is A. Now answer Questions 21 through 30 in the same manner.

21. BYPDTJL 2495308 21.____
PLRDTJU 9815301
DTJRYLK 5207486

22. RPBYRJK 7934706 22.____
PKTYLBU 9624821
KDLPJYR 6489047

23.	TPYBUJR	3942107	23.____
	BYRKPTU	2476931	
	DUKPYDL	5169458	
24.	KBYDLPL	6345898	24.____
	BLRKBRU	2876261	
	JTULDYB	0318542	
25.	LDPYDKR	8594567	25.____
	BDKDRJL	2565708	
	BDRPLUJ	2679810	
26.	PLRLBPU	9858291	26.____
	LPYKRDJ	88936750	
	TDKPDTR	3569527	
27.	RKURPBY	7617924	27.____
	RYUKPTJ	7426930	
	RTKPTJD	7369305	
28.	DYKPBJT	5469203	28.____
	KLPJBTL	6890238	
	TKPLBJP	3698209	
29.	BTPRJYL	2397148	29.____
	LDKUTYR	8561347	
	YDBLRPJ	4528190	
30.	ULPBKYT	1892643	30.____
	KPDTRBJ	6953720	
	YLKJPTB	4860932	

KEY (CORRECT ANSWERS)

1.	A	11.	D	21.	B
2.	C	12.	C	22.	C
3.	A	13.	A	23.	D
4.	D	14.	B	24.	B
5.	C	15.	A	25.	A
6.	C	16.	B	26.	C
7.	C	17.	C	27.	A
8.	D	18.	B	28.	D
9.	A	19.	A	29.	B
10.	B	20.	B	30.	D

RECORD KEEPING

EXAMINATION SECTION

TEST 1

DIRECTIONS: Each question or incomplete statement is followed by several suggested answers or completions. Select the one that BEST answers the question or completes the statement. *PRINT THE LETTER OF THE CORRECT ANSWER IN THE SPACE AT THE RIGHT.*

Questions 1-15.

DIRECTIONS: Questions 1 through 15 are to be answered on the basis of the following list of company names below. Arrange a file alphabetically, word-by-word, disregarding punctuation, conjunctions, and apostrophes. Then answer the questions.

A Bee C Reading Materials
ABCO Parts
A Better Course for Test Preparation
AAA Auto Parts Co.
A-Z Auto Parts, Inc.
Aabar Books
Abbey, Joanne
Boman-Sylvan Law Firm
BMW Autowerks
C Q Service Company
Chappell-Murray, Inc.
E&E Life Insurance
Emcrisco
Gigi Arts
Gordon, Jon & Associates
SOS Plumbing
Schmidt, J.B. Co.

1. Which of these files should appear FIRST? 1.____
   A. ABCO Parts
   B. A Bee C Reading Materials
   C. A Better Course for Test Preparation
   D. AAA Auto Parts Co.

2. Which of these files should appear SECOND? 2.____
   A. A-Z Auto Parts, Inc.
   B. A Bee C Reading Materials
   C. A Better Course for Test Preparation
   D. AAA Auto Parts Co.

3. Which of these files should appear THIRD? 3.____
   A. ABCO Parts
   B. A Bee C Reading Materials
   C. Aabar Books
   D. AAA Auto Parts Co.

4. Which of these files should appear FOURTH? 4.____
   A. Aabar Books
   B. ABCO Parts
   C. Abbey, Joanne
   D. AAA Auto Parts Co.

5. Which of these files should appear LAST? 5.____
   A. Gordon, Jon & Associates
   B. Gigi Arts
   C. Schmidt, J.B. Co.
   D. SOS Plumbing

6. Which of these files should appear between A-Z Auto Parts, Inc. and Abbey, Joanne? 6.____
   A. A Bee C Reading Materials
   B. AAA Auto Parts Co.
   C. ABCO Parts
   D. A Better Course for Test Preparation

7. Which of these files should appear between ABCO Parts and Aabar Books? 7.____
   A. A Bee C Reading Materials
   B. Abbey, Joanne
   C. Aabar Books
   D. A-Z Auto Parts

8. Which of these files should appear between Abbey, Joanne and Boman-Sylvan Law Firm? 8.____
   A. A Better Course for Test Preparation
   B. BMW Autowerks
   C. Chappell-Murray, Inc.
   D. Aabar Books

9. Which of these files should appear between Abbey, Joanne and C Q Service? 9.____
   A. A-Z Auto Parts, Inc.
   B. BMW Autowerks
   C. Choices A and B
   D. Chappell-Murray, Inc.

10. Which of these files should appear between C Q Service Company and Emcrisco? 10.____
   A. Chappell-Murray, Inc.
   B. E&E Life Insurance
   C. Gigi Arts
   D. Choices A and B

11. Which of these files should NOT appear between C Q Service Company and E&E Life Insurance? 11.____
   A. Gordon, Jon & Associates
   B. Emcrisco
   C. Gigi Arts
   D. All of the above

12. Which of these files should appear between Chappell-Murray, Inc. and Gigi Arts? 12.____
    A. C Q Service Inc., E&E Life Insurance, and Emcrisco
    B. Emcrisco, E&E Life Insurance, and Gordon, Jon & Associates
    C. E&E Life Insurance, and Emcrisco
    D. Emcrisco and Gordon, Jon & Associates

13. Which of these files should appear between Gordon, Jon & Associates and SOS Plumbing? 13.____
    A. Gigi Arts
    B. Schmidt,J.B. Co.
    C. Choices A and B
    D. None of the above

14. Each of the choices lists the four files in their proper alphabetical order EXCEPT 14.____
    A. E&E Life Insurance; Gigi Arts; Gordon, Jon & Associates; SOS Plumbing
    B. E&E Life Insurance; Emcrisco; Gigi Arts; SOS Plumbing
    C. Emcrisco; Gordon, Jon & Associates; SOS Plumbing; Schmidt, J.B. Co.
    D. Emcrisco; Gigi Arts; Gordon, Jon & Associates; SOS Plumbing

15. Which of the choices lists the four files in their proper alphabetical order? 15.____
    A. Gigi Arts; Gordon, Jon & Associates; SOS Plumbing; Schmidt, J.B. Co.
    B. Gordon, Jon & Associates; Gigi Arts; Schmidt, J.B. Co.; SOS Plumbing
    C. Gordon, Jon & Associates; Gigi Arts; SOS Plumbing; Schmidt, J.B. Co.
    D. Gigi Arts; Gordon, Jon & Associates; Schmidt, J.B. Co.; SOS Plumbing

16. The alphabetical filing order of two businesses with identical names is determined by the 16.____
    A. length of time each business has been operating
    B. addresses of the businesses
    C. last name of the company president
    D. no one of the above

17. In an alphabetical filing system, if a business name includes a number, it should be 17.____
    A. disregarded
    B. considered a number and placed at the end of an alphabetical section
    C. treated as though it were written in words and alphabetized accordingly
    D. considered a number and placed at the beginning of an alphabetical section

18. If a business name includes a contraction (such as *don't* or *it's*), how should that word be treated in an alphabetical system? 18.____
    A. Divide the word into its separate parts and treat it as two words
    B. Ignore the letters that come after the apostrophe
    C. Ignore the word that contains the contraction
    D. Ignore the apostrophe and consider all letters in the contraction

19. In what order should the parts of an address be considered when using an alphabetical filing system? 19._____
    A. City or town; state; street name; house or building number
    B. State; city or town; street name; house or building number
    C. House or building number; street name; city or town; state
    D. Street name; city or town; state

20. A business record should be cross-referenced when a(n) 20._____
    A. organization is known by an abbreviated name
    B. business has a name change because of a sale, incorporation, or other reason
    C. business is known by a *coined* or common name which differs from a dictionary spelling
    D. all of the above

21. A geographical filing system is MOST effective when 21._____
    A. location is more important than name
    B. many names or titles sound alike
    C. dealing with companies who have offices all over the world
    D. filing personal and business files

Questions 22-25.

DIRECTIONS: Questions 22 through 25 are to be answered on the basis of the list of items below, which are to be filed geographically. Organize the items geographically and then answer the questions.

I. University Press at Berkeley, U.S.
II. Maria Sanchez, Mexico City, Mexico
III. Great Expectations Ltd. in London, England
IV. Justice League, Cape Town, South Africa, Africa
V. Crown Pearls Ltd. in London, England
VI. Joseph Prasad in London, England

22. Which of the following arrangements of the items is composed according to the policy of: *Continent, Country, City, Firm or Individual Name*? 22._____
    A. V, III, IV, VI, II, I
    B. IV, V, III, VI, II, I
    C. I, IV, V, III, VI, II
    D. IV, V, III, VI, I, II

23. Which of the following files is arranged according to the policy of: *Continent, Country, City, Firm or Individual Name*? 23._____
    A. South Africa; Africa; Cape Town; Justice League
    B. Mexico; Mexico City; Maria Sanchez
    C. North America; United States; Berkeley; University Press
    D. England; Europe; London; Prasad, Joseph

24. Which of the following arrangements of the items is composed according to the policy of: *Country, City, Firm or Individual Name*? 24.____
    A. V, VI, III, II, IV, I
    B. I, V, VI, III, II, IV
    C. VI, V, III, II, IV, I
    D. V, III, VI, II, IV, I

25. Which of the following files is arranged according to a policy of: *Country, City, Firm or Individual Name*? 25.____
    A. England; London; Crown Pearls Ltd.
    B. North America; United States; Berkeley; University Press
    C. Africa; Cape Town; Justice League
    D. Mexico City; Mexico; Maria Sanchez

26. Under which of the following circumstances would a phonetic filing system be MOST effective? 26.____
    A. When the person in charge of filing can't spell very well
    B. With large files with names that sound alike
    C. With large files with names that are spelled alike
    D. All of the above

Questions 27-29.

DIRECTIONS: Questions 27 through 29 are to be answered on the basis of the following list of numerical files.

I. 391-023-100
II. 361-132-170
III. 385-732-200
IV. 381-432-150
V. 391-632-387
VI. 361-423-303
VII. 391-123-271

27. Which of the following arrangements of the files follows a consecutive-digit system? 27.____
    A. II, III, IV, I
    B. I, V, VII, III
    C. II, IV, III, I
    D. III, I, V, VII

28. Which of the following arrangements follows a terminal-digit system? 28.____
    A. I, VII, II, IV, III
    B. II, I, IV, V, VII
    C. VII, VI, V, IV, III
    D. I, IV, II, III, VII

29. Which of the following lists follows a middle-digit system? 29.____
    A. I, VII, II, VI, IV, V, III
    B. I, II, VII, IV, VI, V, III
    C. VII, II, I, III, V, VI, IV
    D. VII, I, II, IV, VI, V, III

Questions 30-31.

DIRECTIONS: Questions 30 and 31 are to be answered on the basis of the following information.

I. Reconfirm Laura Bates appointment with James Caldecort on December 12 at 9:30 A.M.
II. Laurence Kinder contact Julia Lucas on August 3 and set up a meeting for week of September 23 at 4 P.M.
III. John Lutz contact Larry Waverly on August 3 and set up appointment for September 23 at 9:30 A.M.
IV. Call for tickets for Gerry Stanton August 21 for New Jersey on September 23, flight 143 at 4:43 P.M.

30. A chronological file for the above information would be 30.____
A. IV, III, II, I B. III, II, IV, I C. IV, II, III, I D. III, I, II, IV

31. Using the above information, a chronological file for the date September 23 would be 31.____
A. II, III, IV B. III, I, IV C. III, II, IV D. IV, III, II

Questions 32-34.

DIRECTIONS: Questions 32 through 34 are to be answered on the basis of the following information.

I. Call Roger Epstein, Ashoke Naipaul, Jon Anderson, and Sara Washingon on April 19 at 1:00 P.M. to set up meeting with Alika D'Ornay for June 6 in New York.
II. Call Martin Ames before noon on April 19 to confirm afternoon meeting with Bob Greenwood on April 20th.
III. Set up meeting room at noon for 2:30 P.M. meeting on April 19th.
IV. Ashley Stanton contact Bob Greenwood at 9:00 A.M. on April 20 and set up meeting for June 6 at 8:30 A.M.
V. Carol Guiland contact Shelby Van Ness during afternoon of April 20 and set up meeting for June 6 at 10:00 A.M.
VI. Call airline and reserve tickets on June 6 for Roger Epstein trip to Denver on July 8.
VII. Meeting at 2:30 P.M. on April 19th.

32. A chronological file for all of the above information would be 32.____
A. II, I, III, VII, V, IV, VI B. III, VII, II, I, IV, V, VI
C. III, VII, I, II, V, IV, VI D. II, III, I, VII, IV, V, VI

33. A chronological file for the date of April 19th would be 33.____
A. II, III, VII, I B. II, III, I, VII C. VII, I, III, II D. III, VII, I, II

34. Add the following information to the file, and then create a chronological file for April 20th: VIII. April 20: 3:00 P.M. meeting between Bob Greenwood and Martin Ames. 34.____
A. IV, V, VIII B. IV, VIII, V C. VIII, V, IV D. V, IV, VIII

35. The PRIMARY advantage of computer records over a manual system is 35.____
A. speed of retrieval
B. accuracy
C. cost
D. potential file loss

KEY (CORRECT ANSWERS)

1.	B	11.	D	21.	A	31.	C
2.	C	12.	C	22.	B	32.	D
3.	D	13.	B	23.	C	33.	B
4.	A	14.	C	24.	D	34.	A
5.	D	15.	D	25.	A	35.	A
6.	C	16.	B	26.	B		
7.	B	17.	C	27.	C		
8.	B	18.	D	28.	D		
9.	C	19.	A	29.	A		
10.	D	20.	D	30.	B		

NAME AND NUMBER CHECKING

EXAMINATION SECTION

TEST 1

DIRECTIONS: This test is designed to measure your speed/and accuracy. You are urged to work both quickly and accurately and to do correctly as many lists as you can in the time allowed. The test consists of lists or pairs of names and numbers. Count the number of IDENTICAL pairs in each list. Then, select the correct number, 1, 2, 3, 4, 5, and indicate your choice in the space at the right. Two sample questions are presented for your guidance, together with the correct solutions.

<u>SAMPLE LIST A</u>
Adelphi College – Adelphia College
Braxton Corp – Braxeton Corp.
Wassaic State School – Wassaic State School
Central Islip State Hospital – Central Isllip State Hospital
Greenwich House – Greenwich House

NOTE: There are only two correct pairs—Wassaic State School and Greenwich House. Therefore, the CORRECT answer is 2.

<u>SAMPLE LIST B</u>
78453694 – 78453684
784530 – 784530
533 – 534
67845 – 67845
2368745 – 2368755

NOTE: There are only two correct pairs—784530 and 67845. Therefore, the CORRECT answer is 2.

<u>LIST 1</u> 1.____

Diagnostic Clinic – Diagnostic Clinic
Yorkville Health – Yorkville Health
Meinhard Clinic – Meinhart Clinic
Corlears Clinic – Carlears Clinic
Tremont Diagnostic – Tremont Diagnostic

<u>LIST 2</u> 2.____

73526 – 73526
7283627198 – 7283627198
627 – 637
728352617283 – 7283526178282
6281 – 6281

LIST 3		3.____
Jefferson Clinic	– Jeffersen Clinic	
Mott Haven Center	– Mott Havan Center	
Bronx Hospital	– Bronx Hospital	
Montefiore Hospital	– Montifeore Hospital	
Beth Isreal Hospital	– Beth Israel Hospital	
LIST 4		4.____
936271826	– 936371826	
5271	– 5291	
82637192037	– 82637192037	
527182	– 5271882	
726354256	- 72635456	
LIST 5		5.____
Trinity Hospital	– Trinity Hospital	
Central Harlem	– Centrel Harlem	
St. Luke's Hospital	– St. Lukes' Hospital	
Mt. Sinai Hospital	– Mt. Sinia Hospital	
N.Y. Dispensery	– N.Y. Dispensary	
LIST 6		6.____
725361552637	– 725361555637	
7526378	– 7526377	
6975	– 6975	
82637481028	– 82637481028	
3427	– 3429	
LIST 7		7.____
Misericordia Hospital	– Miseracordia Hospital	
Lebonan Hospital	– Lebanon Hospital	
Gouverneur Hospital	– Gouverner Hospital	
German Polyclinic	– German Policlinic	
French Hospital	– French Hospital	
LIST 8		8.____
8277364933251	– 827364933351	
63728	– 63728	
367281	– 367281	
62733846273	– 6273846293	
62836	- 6283	
LIST 9		9.____
King's County Hospital	– Kings County Hospital	
St. Johns Long Island	– St. John's Long Island	
Bellevue Hospital	– Bellvue Hospital	
Beth David Hospital	– Beth David Hospital	
Samaritan Hospital	– Samariton Hospital	

LIST 10 10.____

62836454	– 62836455
42738267	– 42738369
573829	– 573829
738291627874	– 738291627874
725	- 735

LIST 11 11.____

Bloomingdal Clinic	– Bloomingdale Clinic
Communitty Hospital	– Community Hospital
Metroplitan Hospital	– Metropoliton Hospital
Lenox Hill Hospital	– Lonex Hill Hospital
Lincoln Hospital	– Lincoln Hospital

LIST 12 12.____

6283364728	– 6283648
627385	– 627383
54283902	– 54283602
63354	– 63354
7283562781	- 7283562781

LIST 13 13.____

Sydenham Hospital	– Sydanham Hospital
Roosevalt Hospital	– Roosevelt Hospital
Vanderbilt Clinic	– Vanderbild Clinic
Women's Hospital	– Woman's Hospital
Flushing Hospital	– Flushing Hospital

LIST 14 14.____

62738	– 62738
727355542321	– 72735542321
263849332	– 263849332
262837	– 263837
47382912	- 47382922

LIST 15 15.____

Episcopal Hospital	– Episcapal Hospital
Flower Hospital	– Flouer Hospital
Stuyvesent Clinic	– Stuyvesant Clinic
Jamaica Clinic	– Jamaica Clinic
Ridgwood Clinic	– Ridgewood Clinic

LIST 16 16.____

628367299	– 628367399
111	– 111
118293304829	– 1182839489
4448	– 4448
333693678	- 333693678

LIST 17 17.____

Arietta Crane Farm	– Areitta Crane Farm
Bikur Chilim Home	– Bikur Chilom Home
Burke Foundation	– Burke Foundation
Blythedale Home	– Blythdale Home
Campbell Cottages	– Cambell Cottages

LIST 18 18.____

32123	– 32132
273893326783	– 27389326783
473829	– 473829
7382937	– 7383937
3628890122332	- 36289012332

LIST 19 19.____

Caraline Rest	– Caroline Rest
Loreto Rest	– Loretto Rest
Edgewater Creche	– Edgwater Creche
Holiday Farm	– Holiday Farm
House of St. Giles	– House of st. Giles

LIST 20 20.____

557286777	– 55728677
3678902	– 3678892
1567839	– 1567839
7865434712	– 7865344712
9927382	- 9927382

LIST 21 21.____

Isabella Home	– Isabela Home
James A. Moore Home	– James A. More Home
The Robin's Nest	– The Roben's Nest
Pelham Home	– Pelam Home
St. Eleanora's Home	– St. Eleanora's Home

LIST 22 22.____

273648293048	– 273648293048
334	– 334
7362536478	– 7362536478
7362819273	– 7362819273
7362	- 7363

LIST 23 23.____

St. Pheobe's Mission	– St. Phebe's Mission
Seaside Home	– Seaside Home
Speedwell Society	– Speedwell Society
Valeria Home	– Valera Home
Wiltwyck	- Wildwyck

LIST 24 24.____

63728	– 63738
63728192736	– 63728192738
428	– 458
62738291527	– 62738291529
63728192	- 63728192

LIST 25 25.____

McGaffin	– McGafin
David Ardslee	– David Ardslee
Axton Supply	– Axeton Supply Co
Alice Russell	– Alice Russell
Dobson Mfg. Co.	– Dobsen Mfg. Co.

KEY (CORRECT ANSWERS)

1.	3	11.	1
2.	3	12.	2
3.	1	13.	1
4.	1	14.	2
5.	1	15.	1
6.	2	16.	3
7.	1	17.	1
8.	2	18.	1
9.	1	19.	1
10.	2	20.	2

21.	1
22.	4
23.	2
24.	1
25.	2

TEST 2

DIRECTIONS: This test is designed to measure your speed/and accuracy. You are urged to work both quickly and accurately and to do correctly as many lists as you can in the time allowed. The test consists of lists or pairs of names and numbers. Count the number of IDENTICAL pairs in each list. Then, select the correct number, 1, 2, 3, 4, 5, and indicate your choice in the space at the right.

LIST 1 — 1.____

82637381028	– 82637281028
928	– 928
72937281028	– 72937281028
7362	– 7362
927382615	– 927382615

LIST 2 — 2.____

Albee Theatre	– Albee Theatre
Lapland Lumber Co.	– Laplund Lumber Co.
Adelphi College	– Adelphi College
Jones & Son Inc.	– Jones & Sons Inc.
S.W. Ponds Co.	– S.W. Ponds Co.

LIST 3 — 3.____

85345	– 85345
895643278	– 895643277
726352	– 726353
632685	– 632685
7263524	– 7236524

LIST 4 — 4.____

Eagle Library	– Eagle Library
Dodge Ltd.	– Dodge Co.
Stromberg Carlson	– Stromberg Carlsen
Clairice Ling	– Clairice Linng
Mason Book Co.	– Matson Book Co.

LIST 5 — 5.____

66273	– 66273
629	– 629
7382517283	– 7382517283
637281	– 639281
2738261	– 2788261

LIST 6 — 6.____

Robert MacColl	– Robert McColl
Buick Motor	– Buck Motors
Murray Bay & Co. Ltd.	– Murray Bay Co. Ltd.
L.T. Ltyle	– L.T. Lyttle
A.S. Landas	– A.S. Landas

LIST 7		7.____
6271526374890	– 627152637490	
73526189	– 73526189	
5372	– 5392	
637281142	– 63728124	
4783946	– 4783046	
LIST 8		8.____
Tyndall Burke	– Tyndell Burke	
W. Briehl	– W. Briehl	
Burritt Publishing Co.	– Buritt Publishing Co.	
Frederick Breyer & Co.	– Frederick Breyer Co.	
Bailey Buulard	– Bailey Bullard	
LIST 9		9.____
634	– 634	
16837	– 163837	
273892223678	– 27389223678	
527182	– 527782	
3628901223	– 3629002223	
LIST 10		10.____
Ernest Boas	– Ernest Boas	
Rankin Barne	– Rankin Barnes	
Edward Appley	– Edward Appely	
Camel	– Camel	
Caiger Food Co.	– Caiger Food Co.	
LIST 11		11.____
6273	– 6273	
322	– 332	
15672839	– 15672839	
63728192637	– 63728192639	
738	– 738	
LIST 12		12.____
Wells Fargo Co.	– Wells Fargo Co.	
W.D. Brett	– W.D. Britt	
Tassco Co.	– Tassko Co.	
Republic Mills	– Republic Mill	
R.W. Burnham	– R.W. Burhnam	
LIST 13		13.____
7253529152	– 7283529152	
6283	– 6383	
52839102738	– 5283910238	
308	– 398	
82637201927	– 8263720127	

LIST 14		14.____
Schumacker Co.	– Shumacker Co.	
C.H. Caiger	– C.H. Caiger	
Abraham Strauss	– Abram Straus	
B.F. Boettjer	– B.F. Boettijer	
Cut-Rate Store	– Cut-Rate Stores	
LIST 15		15.____
15273826	– 15273826	
72537	– 73537	
726391027384	– 62639107384	
637389	– 627399	
725382910	– 725382910	
LIST 16		16.____
Hixby Ltd.	– Hixby Lt'd.	
S. Reiner	– S. Riener	
Reynard Co.	– Reynord Co.	
Esso Gassoline Co.	– Esso Gasolene Co.	
Belle Brock	– Belle Brock	
LIST 17		17.____
7245	– 7245	
819263728192	– 819263728172	
682537289	– 682537298	
789	– 789	
82936542891	– 82936542891	
LIST 18		18.____
Joseph Cartwright	– Joseph Cartwrite	
Foote Food Co.	– Foot Food Co.	
Weiman & Held	– Weiman & Held	
Sanderson Shoe Co.	– Sandersen Shoe Co.	
A.M. Byrne	– A.N. Byrne	
LIST 19		19.____
4738267	– 4738277	
63728	– 63729	
6283628901	– 6283628991	
918264	– 918264	
263728192037	– 2637728192073	
LIST 20		20.____
Exray Laboratories	– Exray Labratories	
Curley Toy Co.	– Curly Toy Co.	
J. Lauer & Cross	– J. Laeur & Cross	
Mireco Brands	– Mireco Brands	
Sandor Lorand	– Sandor Larand	

LIST 21		21.____
607	– 609	
6405	– 6403	
976	– 996	
101267	– 101267	
2065432	– 20965432	
LIST 22		22.____
John Macy & Sons	– John Macy & Son	
Venus Pencil Co.	– Venus Pencil Co.	
Nell McGinnis	– Nell McGinnis	
McCutcheon & Co.	– McCutcheon & Co.	
Sun-Tan Oil	– Sun-Tan Oil	
LIST 23		23.____
703345700	– 703345700	
46754	– 466754	
3367490	– 3367490	
3379	– 3778	
47384	– 47394	
LIST 24		24.____
arthritis	– arthritis	
asthma	– asthma	
endocrine	– endocrene	
gastro-enterological	– gastrol-enteralogical	
orthopedic	– orthopedic	
LIST 25		25.____
743829432	– 743828432	
998	– 998	
732816253902	– 732816252902	
46829	– 46830	
7439120249	– 7439210249	

KEY (CORRECT ANSWERS)

1.	4	11.	3
2.	3	12.	1
3.	2	13.	1
4.	1	14.	1
5.	2	15.	2
6.	1	16.	1
7.	2	17.	3
8.	1	18.	1
9.	1	19.	1
10.	3	20.	1
21.	1		
22.	4		
23.	2		
24.	3		
25.	1		

NAME AND NUMBER COMPARISONS

COMMENTARY

This test seeks to measure your ability and disposition to do a job carefully and accurately, your attention to exactness and preciseness of detail, your alertness and versatility in discerning similarities and differences between things, and your power in systematically handling written language symbols.

It is actually a test of your ability to do academic and/or clerical work, using the basic elements of verbal (qualitative) and mathematical (quantitative) learning—words and numbers.

EXAMINATION SECTION

TEST 1

DIRECTIONS: Questions 1 through 6 consist of sets of names and addresses. In each question, the name and address in Column II should be an exact copy of the name and address in Column II. *PRINT IN THE SPACE AT THE RIGHT THE LETTER*

A. if there is a mistake only in the name
B. if there is a mistake only in the address
C. if there is a mistake in both name and address
D. If there is no mistake in either name or address

SAMPLE:

Michael Filbert 456 Reade Street New York, N.Y. 10013	Michael Filbert 644 Reade Street New York, N.Y. 10013

Since there is a mistake only in the address, the answer is B.

1.	Esta Wong 141 West 68 St. New York, N.Y. 10023	Esta Wang 141 West 68 St. New York, N.Y. 10023	1.____
2.	Dr. Alberto Grosso 3475 12th Avenue Brooklyn, N.Y. 11218	Dr. Alberto Grosso 3475 12th Avenue Brooklyn, N.Y. 11218	2.____
3.	Mrs. Ruth Bortlas 482 Theresa Ct. Far Rockaway, N.Y. 11691	Ms. Ruth Bortias 482 Theresa Ct. Far Rockaway, N.Y. 11169	3.____
4.	Mr. and Mrs. Howard Fox 2301 Sedgwick Ave. Bronx, N.Y. 10468	Mr. and Mrs. Howard Fox 231 Sedgwick Ave. Bronx, N.Y. 10468	4.____
5.	Miss Marjorie Black 223 East 23 Street New York, N.Y. 10010	Miss Margorie Black 223 East 23 Street New York, N.Y. 10010	5.____

6.	Michelle Herman 806 Valley Rd. Old Tappan, N.J. 07675	Michelle Hermann 806 Valley Dr. Old Tappan, N.J. 07675	6.____

KEY (CORRECT ANSWERS)

1. A
2. D
3. C
4. B
5. A
6. C

TEST 2

DIRECTIONS: Questions 1 through 6 consist of sets of names and addresses. In each question, the name and address in Column II should be an exact copy of the name and address in Column II. *PRINT IN THE SPACE AT THE RIGHT THE LETTER*

A. if there is a mistake only in the name
B. if there is a mistake only in the address
C. if there is a mistake in both name and address
D. If there is no mistake in either name or address

1.	Ms. Joan Kelly 313 Franklin Ave. Brooklyn, N.Y. 11202	Ms. Joan Kielly 318 Franklin Ave. Brooklyn, N.Y. 11202	1.____
2.	Mrs. Eileen Engel 47-24 86 Road Queens, N.Y. 11122	Mrs. Ellen Engel 47-24 86 Road Queens, N.Y. 11122	2.____
3.	Marcia Michaels 213 E. 81 St. New York, N.Y. 10012	Marcia Michaels 213 E. 81 St. New York, N.Y. 10012	3.____
4.	Rev. Edward J. Smyth 1401 Brandeis Street San Francisco, Calif. 96201	Rev. Edward J. Smyth 1401 Brandies Street San Francisco, Calif. 96201	4.____
5.	Alicia Rodriguez 24-68 81 St. Elmhurst, N.Y. 11122	Alicia Rodriquez 2468 81 St. Elmhurst, N.Y. 11122	5.____
6.	Ernest Eissemann 21 Columbia St. New York, N.Y. 10007	Ernest Eisermann 21 Columbia St. New York, N.Y. 10007	6.____

KEY (CORRECT ANSWERS)

1. C
2. A
3. D
4. B
5. C
6. A

TEST 3

DIRECTIONS: Questions 1 through 8 consist of names, locations, and telephone numbers. In each question, the name, location and number in Column II should be an exact copy of the name, location, and number in Column I. *PRINT IN THE SPACE AT THE RIGHT THE LETTER*

A. if there is a mistake in one line only
B. if there is a mistake in two lines only
C. if there is a mistake in three lines only
D. if there are no mistakes in any of the lines

	Column I	Column II	
1.	Ruth Lang EAM Bldg., Room C101 625-2000, ext. 765	Ruth Lang EAM Bldg., Room C110 625-2000, ext. 765	1.____
2.	Anne Marie Ionozzi Investigations, Room 827 576-4000, ext. 832	Anna Marie Ionozzi Investigation, Room 827 566-4000, ext. 832	2.____
3.	Willard Jameson Fm C Bldg. Room 687 454-3010	Willard Jamieson Fm C Bldg. Room 687 454-3010	3.____
4.	Joanne Zimmermann Bldg. SW, Room 314 532-4601	Joanne Zimmermann Bldg. SW, Room 314 532-4601	4.____
5.	Carlyle Whetstone Payroll Division-A, Room 212A 262-5000, ext. 471	Caryle Whetstone Payroll Division-A, Room 212A 262-5000, ext. 417	5.____
6.	Kenneth Chiang Legal Council, Room 9745 (201) 416-9100, ext. 17	Kenneth Chiang Legal Counsel, Room 9745 (201) 416-9100, ext. 17	6.____
7.	Ethel Koenig Personnel Services Div, Rm 433 635-7572	Ethel Hoenig Personal Services Div, Rm 433 635-7527	7.____
8.	Joyce Ehrhardt Office of Administrator, Rm W56 387-8706	Joyce Ehrhart Office of Administrator, Rm W56 387-7806	8.____

KEY (CORRECT ANSWERS)

1.	A	6.	A
2.	C	7.	C
3.	A	8.	B
4.	D		
5.	B		

TEST 4

DIRECTIONS: Each of Questions 1 through 10 gives the identification number and name of a person who has received treatment at a certain hospital. You are to choose the option (A, B, C, or D) which has EXACTLY the same number and name as those given in the question.

SAMPLE QUESTION:
123765 Frank Y. Jones
A. 123675 Frank Y. Jones
B. 123765 Frank T. Jones
C. 123765 Frank Y. Jones
D. 123765 Frank Y. Jones

The correct answer is D, because it is the only option showing the identification number and name exactly as they are in the sample question.

1. 754898 Diane Malloy 1.____
A. 745898 Diane Malloy
B. 754898 Dion Malloy
C. 754898 Diane Malloy
D. 754898 Diane Maloy

2. 661818 Ferdinand Figueroa 2.____
A. 661818 Ferdinand Figeuroa
B. 661618 Ferdinand Figueroa
C. 661818 Ferdnand Figueroa
D. 661818 Ferdinand Figueroa

3. 100101 Norman D. Braustein 3.____
A. 100101 Norman D. Braustein
B. 101001 Norman D. Braustein
C. 100101 Norman P. Braustien
D. 100101 Norman D. Bruastein

4. 838696 Robert Kittredge 4.____
A. 838969 Robert Kittredge
B. 838696 Robert Kittredge
C. 388696 Robert Kittredge
D. 838696 Robert Kittridge

5. 243716 Abraham Soletsky 5.____
A. 243716 Abrahm Soletsky
B. 243716 Abraham Solestky
C. 243176 Abraham Soletsky
D. 243716 Abraham Soletsky

6. 981121 Phillip M. Maas 6.____
A. 981121 Phillip M. Mass
B. 981211 Phillip M. Maas
C. 981121 Phillip M. Maas
D. 981121 Phillip N. Maas

7. 786556 George Macalusso 7.____
A. 785656 George Macalusso
B. 786556 George Macalusso
C. 786556 George Maculusso
D. 786556 George Macluasso

8. 639472 Eugene Weber 8.____
A. 639472 Eugene Weber
B. 639472 Eugene Webre
C. 693472 Eugene Weber
D. 639742 Eugene Weber

9. 724936 John J. Lomonaco 9.____
   A. 724936 John J. Lomanoco
   B. 724396 John L. Lomonaco
   C. 7224936 John J. Lomonaco
   D. 724936 John J. Lamonaco

10. 899868 Michael Schnitzer 10.____
   A. 899868 Micheal Schnitzer
   B. 898968 Michael Schnizter
   C. 899688 Michael Schnitzer
   D. 899868 Michael Schnitzer

KEY (CORRECT ANSWERS)

1.	C	6.	C
2.	D	7.	B
3.	A	8.	A
4.	B	9.	C
5.	D	10.	D

CODING

EXAMINATION SECTION

TEST 1

COMMENTARY

An ingenious question-type called coding, involving elements of alphabetizing, filing, name and number comparison, and evaluative judgment and application, has currently won wide acceptance in testing circles for measuring clerical aptitude and general ability, particularly on the senior (middle) grades (levels).

While the directions for this question-type usually vary in detail, the candidate is generally asked to consider groups of names, codes, and numbers, and, then, according to a given plan, to arrange codes in alphabetic order; to arrange these in numerical sequence; to rearrange columns of names and numbers in correct order; to espy errors in coding; to choose the correct coding arrangement in consonance with the given directions and examples, etc.

This question-type appears to have few parameters in respect to form, substance, or degree of difficulty.

Accordingly, acquaintance with, and practice in the coding question is recommended for the serious candidate.

DIRECTIONS: Column I consists of serial numbers of dollar bills. Column II shows different ways of arranging the corresponding serial numbers.
The serial numbers of dollar bills in Column I begin and end with a capital letter and have an eight-digit number in between. The serial numbers in Column I are to be arranged according to the following rules:
First: In alphabetical order according to the first letter.
Second: When two or more serial numbers have the same first letter, in alphabetical order according to the last letter.
Third: When two or more serial numbers have the same first and last letters, in numerical order, beginning with the lowest number.

The serial numbers in Column I are numbered (1) through (5) in the order in which they are listed. In Column II, the numbers (1) through (5) are arranged in four different ways to show different arrangements of the corresponding serial numbers. Choose the answer in Column II in which the serial numbers are arranged according to the above rules.

Column I	Column II
1. E75044127B	A. 4, 1, 3, 2, 5
2. B96399104A	B. 4, 1, 2, 3, 5
3. B93939086A	C. 4, 3, 2, 5, 1
4. B47064465H	D. 3, 2, 5, 4, 1

In the simple question, the four serial numbers starting with B should be put before the serial number starting with E. The serial numbers starting with B and ending with A should be put before the serial number starting with B and ending with H. The three serial numbers starting with B and ending with A should be listed in numerical order, beginning with the lowest number. The correct way to arrange the serial numbers, therefore, is:

3. B93939086A
2. B96399104A
5. B99040922A
4. B47064465H
1. E75044127B

Since the order of arrangement is 3, 2, 5, 4, 1, the answer to the sample question is D.

	Column I	Column II	
1.	1. D89143888P 2. D98143838B 3. D89113883B 4. D89148338P 5. D89148388B	A. 3, 5, 2, 1, 4 B. 3, 1, 4, 5, 2 C. 4, 2, 3, 1, 5 D. 4, 1, 3, 5, 2	1.____
2.	1. W62455590E 2. W62455090F 3. W62405099E 4. V62455097F 5. V62405979E	A. 2, 4, 3, 1, 5 B. 3, 1, 5, 2, 4 C. 5, 3, 1, 4, 2 D. 5, 4, 3, 1, 2	2.____
3.	1. N74663826M 2. M74633286M 3. N76633228N 4. M76483686N 5. M74636688M	A. 2, 4, 5, 3, 1 B. 2, 5, 4, 1, 3 C. 1, 2, 5, 3, 4 D. 2, 5, 1, 4, 3	3.____
4.	1. P97560324B 2. R97663024B 3. P97503024E 4. R97563240E 5. P97652304B	A. 1, 5, 2, 3, 4 B. 3, 1, 4, 5, 2 C. 1, 5, 3, 2, 4 D. 1, 5, 2, 3, 4	4.____
5.	1. H92411165G 2. A92141465G 3. H92141165C 4. H92444165C 5. A92411465G	A. 2, 5, 3, 4, 1 B. 3, 4, 2, 5, 1 C. 3, 2, 1, 5, 4 D. 3, 1, 2, 5, 4	5.____
6.	1. X90637799S 2. N90037696S 3. Y90677369B 4. X09677693B 5. M09673699S	A. 4, 3, 5, 2, 1 B. 5, 4, 2, 1, 3 C. 5, 2, 4, 1, 3 D. 5, 2, 3, 4, 1	6.____

Column I	Column II	
7. 1. K78425174L	A. 4, 2, 1, 3, 5	7.____
2. K78452714C	B. 2, 3, 5, 4, 1	
3. K78547214N	C. 1, 4, 2, 3, 5	
4. K78442774C	D. 4, 2, 1, 5, 3	
5. K78547724M		
8. 1. P18736652U	A. 1, 3, 4, 5, 2	8.____
2. P18766352V	B. 1, 5, 2, 3, 4	
3. T17686532U	C. 3, 4, 5, 1, 2	
4. T17865523U	D. 5, 2, 1, 3, 4	
5. P18675332V		
9. 1. L51138101K	A. 1, 5, 3, 2, 4	9.____
2. S51138001R	B. 1, 3, 5, 2, 4	
3. S51188222K	C. 1, 5, 1, 4, 3	
4. S51183110R	D. 2, 5, 1, 4, 3	
5. L51188100R		
10. 1. J28475336	A. 5, 1, 2, 3, 4	10.____
2. T28775363D	B. 4, 3, 5, 1, 2	
3. J27843566P	C. 1, 5, 2, 4, 3	
4. T27834563P	D. 5, 1, 3, 2, 4	
5. J2843553D		
11. 1. S55126179E	A. 1, 5, 2, 3, 4	11.____
2. R51336177Q	B. 3, 4, 1, 5, 2	
3. P55126177R	C. 3, 5, 2, 1, 4	
4. S55126178R	D. 4, 3, 1, 5, 2	
5. R55126180P		
12. 1. T64217813Q	A. 4, 1, 3, 2, 4	12.____
2. I64217817O	B. 2, 4, 3, 1, 5	
3. T64217818O	C. 4, 1, 5, 2, 3	
4. I64217811Q	D. 2, 3, 4, 1, 5	
5. T64217816Q		
13. 1. B33886897B	A. 5, 1, 3, 4, 2	13.____
2. B38386882B	B. 1, 2, 5, 3, 4	
3. D33389862B	C. 1, 2, 5, 4, 3	
4. D33336887D	D. 2, 1, 4, 5, 3	
5. B38888697D		
14. 1. E11664554M	A. 4, 1, 2, 5, 3	14.____
2. F11164544M	B. 2, 4, 1, 5, 3	
3. F11614455N	C. 4, 2, 1, 3, 5	
4. E11665454M	D. 1, 4, 2, 3, 5	
5. F16161545N		

	Column I	Column II	
15.	1. C86611355W 2. C68631533V 3. G88631533V 4. C68833515V 5. G68833511W	A. 2, 4, 1, 5, 3 B. 1, 2, 4, 3, 5 C. 1, 2, 5, 4, 3 D. 1, 2, 4, 3, 5	15.____
16.	1. R73665312J 2. P73685512J 3. P73968511J 4. R73665321K 5. R63985211K	A. 3, 2, 1, 4, 5 B. 2, 3, 5, 1, 4 C. 2, 3, 1, 5, 4 D. 3, 1, 5, 2, 4	16.____
17.	1. X33661222U 2. Y83961323V 3. Y88991123V 4. X33691233U 5. X38691333U	A. 1, 4, 5, 2, 3 B. 4, 5, 1, 3, 2 C. 4, 5, 1, 2, 3 D. 4, 1, 5, 2, 3	17..____
18.	1. B22838847W 2. B28833874V 3. B22288344X 4. B28238374V 5. B28883347V	A. 4, 5, 2, 3, 1 B. 4, 2, 5, 1, 3 C. 4, 5, 2, 1, 3 D. 4, 1, 5, 2, 3	18.____
19.	1. H44477447G 2. H47444777G 3. H74777477C 4. H44747447G 5. H77747447C	A. 1, 3, 5, 4, 2 B. 3, 1, 5, 2, 4 C. 1, 4, 2, 3, 5 D. 3, 5, 1, 4, 2	19.____
20.	1. G11143447G 2. G15133388C 3. C15134378G 4. G11534477C 5. C15533337C	A. 3, 5, 1, 4, 2 B. 1, 4, 3, 2, 5 C. 5, 3, 4, 2, 1 D. 4, 3, 1, 2, 5	20.____
21.	1. J96693369F 2. J66939339F 3. J96693693E 4. J966T3933E 5. J69639363F	A. 4, 3, 2, 5, 1 B. 2, 5, 4, 1, 3 C. 2, 5, 4, 3, 1 D. 3, 4, 5, 2, 1	21.____
22.	1. L15567834Z 2. P11587638Z 3. M51567688Z 4. O55578784Z 5. N53588783Z	A. 3, 1, 5, 2, 4 B. 1, 3, 5, 4, 2 C. 1, 3, 5, 2, 4 D. 3, 1, 4, 4, 2	22.____

	Column I	Column II	
23.	1. C83261824G 2. C78361822C 3. G83261732G 4. C88261823C 5. G83261743C	A. 2, 4, 1, 5, 3 B. 4, 2, 1, 3, 5 C. 3, 1, 5, 2, 4 D. , 3, 5, 1, 4	23.____
24.	1. A11710107H 2. H17110017A 3. A11170707A 4. H17170171H 5. A11710177A	A. 2, 1, 4, 3, 5 B. 3, 1, 5, 2, 4 C. 3, 4, 1, 5, 2 D. 3, 5, 1, 2, 4	24.____
25.	1. R26794821S 2. O26794821T 3. M26794821Z 4. Q26794821R 5. S26794821P	A. 3, 2, 4, 1, 5 B. 3, 4, 2, 1, 5 C. 4, 2, 1, 3, 5 D. 5, 4, 1, 2, 3	25.____

KEY (CORRECT ANSWERS)

1. A
2. D
3. B
4. C
5. A

6. C
7. D
8. B
9. A
10. D

11. C
12. B
13. B
14. D
15. A

16. C
17. A
18. B
19. D
20. C

21. A
22. B
23. A
24. D
25. A

TEST 2

Questions 1-5.

DIRECTIONS: Questions 1 through 5 consist of a set of letters and numbers located under Column I. For each question, pick the answer (A, B, C, or D) located under Column II which contains ONLY letters and numbers that appear in the question in Column II. *PRINT THE LETTER OF THE CORRECT ANSWER IN THE SPACE AT THE RIGHT.*

SAMPLE QUESTION

Column I	Column II
B-9-P-H-2-Z-N-8-4-M	A. B-4-C-3-R-9 B. 4-H-P-8-6-N C. P-2-Z-8-M-9 D. 4-B-N-5-E-Z

Choice C is the correct answer because P,2,Z,8,M and 9 all appear in the sample question. All the other choices have at least one letter or number that is not in the question.

	Column I	Column II	
1.	1-7-6-J-L-T-3-S-A-2	A. J-3-S-A-7-L B. T-S-A-2-6-5 C. 3-7-J-L-S-Z D. A-7-4-J-L-1	1.____
2.	C-0-Q-5-3-9-H-L-2-7	A. F-9-T-2-7-Q B. 3-0-6-9-L-C C. 9-L-7-Q-C-3 D. H-Q-4-5-9-7	2.____
3.	P-3-B-C-5-6-0-E-1-T	A. B-4-6-1-3-T B. T-B-P-3-E-0 C. 5-3-0-E-B-G D. 0-6-P-T-9-B	3.____
4.	U-T-Z-2-4-S-8-6-B-3	A. 2-4-S-V-Z-3 B. B-Z-S-8-3-6 C. 4-T-U-8-L-B D. 9-3-T-Z-1-2	4.____
5.	4-D-F-G-C-6-8-3-J-L	A. T-D-6-8-4-J B. C-4-3-2-J-F C. 8-3-C-5-G-6 D. C-8-6-J-G-L	5.____

Questions 6-12.

DIRECTIONS: Each of the questions numbered 6 through 12 consist of a long series of letters and numbers under Column I and four short series of letters and numbers under Column II. For each question, choose the short series of letters and numbers which is entirely and exactly the same as some part of the long series.

Column I	Column II	
6. IE227FE383L4700	A. E27FE3 B. EF838L C. EL4700 D. 83LE70	6.____
7. 77J646G54NPB318	A. NPB318 B. J646J5 C. 4G54NP D. C54NPB	7.____
8. 85887T358W24A93	A. 858887 B. W24A93 C. 858W24 D. 87T353	8.____
9. E104RY796B33H14	A. 04RY79 B. E14RYR C. 96B3H1 D. RY7996	9.____
10. W58NP12141DE07M	A. 8MP121 B. W58NP1 C. 14DEO7 D. 12141D	10.____
11. P473R365M442V5W	A. P47365 B. 73P365 C. 365M44 D. 5X42V5	11.____
12. 865CG441V21SS59	A. 1V12SS B. V21SS5 C. 5GC441 D. 894CG4	12.____

KEY (CORRECT ANSWERS)

1.	A	7.	A
2.	C	8.	B
3.	B	9.	A
4.	B	10.	D
5.	D	11.	C
6	D	12.	B

TEST 3

DIRECTIONS: Each question from 1 through 8 consists of a set of letters and numbers. For each question, pick as your answer from the column to the right the choice has ONLY numbers and letters that are in the question you are answering.

To help you understand what to do, the following sample question is given:

SAMPLE: B-9-P-H-2-Z-N-8-4-M

A. B-4-C-3-E-9
B. 4-H-P-8-6-N
C. P-2-Z-8-M-9
D. 4-B-N-R-E-A

Choice C is the correct answer because P, 2, Z, 8, M-9 are in the sample question. All the other choices have at least one letter or number that is not in the question.

Questions 1 through 4 are based on Column I.

		Column I	
1.	X-8-3-I-H-9-4-G-P-U	A. I-G-W-8-2-1	1.____
2.	4-1-2-X-U-B-9-H-7-3	B. U-3-G-9-P-8	2.____
3.	U-I-G-2-5-4-W-P-3-B	C. 3-G-I-4-S-U	3.____
4.	3-H-7-G-4-5-1-U-B	D. 9-X-4-7-2-H	4.____

Questions 5 through 8 are based on Column II.

		Column II	
5.	L-2-9-Z-R-8-Q-Y-5-7	A. 8-R-N-3-T-Z	5.____
6.	J-L-9-N-Y-8-5-Q-Z-2	B. 2-L-R-5-7-Q	6.____
7.	T-Y-3-3-J-Q-2-N-R-Z	C. J-2-8-Z-T-5	7.____
8.	8-Z-7-T-N-L-1-E-R-3	D. Z-8-9-3-L-5	8.____

KEY (CORRECT ANSWERS)

1.	B	5.	B
2.	D	6.	C
3.	C	7.	A
4.	C	8.	A

TEST 4

DIRECTIONS: Questions 1 through 5 have lines of letters and numbers. Each letter should be matched with its number in accordance with the following table.

Letter:	F	R	C	A	W	L	E	N	B	T
Matching Number:	0	1	2	3	4	5	6	7	8	9

From the table you can determine that the letter F has the matching number 0 below it, the letter R has the matching number 1 below it, etc.

For each question, compare each line of letters and numbers carefully to see if each letter has its correct matching number. If all the letters and numbers are matched correctly in none of the line of the question, mark your answer A; only one of the lines in the question, mark your answer B; only two of the lines of the question, mark your answer C; all three lines of the question, mark your answer D.

WBCR	4826
TLBF	9580
ATNE	3986

There is a mistake in the first line because the letter R should have its matching number 1 instead of the number 6. The second line is correct because each letter shown has the correct matching number.

There is a mistake in the third line because the letter N should have the matching number 7 instead of the number 8. Since all the letters and numbers are matched correctly in only one of the lines in the sample, the correct answer is B.

1.	EBCT	6829	1.____
	ATWR	3962	
	NLBW	7584	
2.	RNCT	1729	2.____
	LNCR	5728	
	WAEB	5368	
3.	STWB	7948	3.____
	RABL	1385	
	TAEF	9360	
4.	LWRB	5417	4.____
	RLWN	1647	
	CBWA	2843	
5.	ABTC	3792	5.____
	WCER	5261	
	AWCN	3417	

KEY (CORRECT ANSWERS)

1. C
2. B
3. D
4. B
5. A

TEST 5

DIRECTIONS: Assume that each of the capital letters in the table below represents the name of an employee enrolled in the city employees' retirement system. The number directly beneath the letter represents the agency for which the employee works, and the small letter directly beneath represents the code for the employee's account.

Name of Employee:	L	O	T	Q	A	M	R	N	C
Agency:	3	4	5	9	8	7	52	1	6
Account Code:	r	f	b	i	d	t	g	e	n

In each of the following Questions 1 through 10, the agency code numbers and the account code letters in Columns 2 and 3 should correspond to the capital letters in Column 1 and should be in the same consecutive order. For each question, look at each column carefully and mark your answer as follows:

if there are one or more errors in Column 2 only, mark your answer A;
if there are one or more errors in Column 3 only, mark your answer B;
if there are one or more error in Column 2 and one or more errors in Column 3, mark your answer C;
if there are NO errors in either column, mark your answer D.

The following sample question is given to help you understand the procedure.

Column 1	Column 2	Column 3
TQLMOC	583746	birtfn

In Column 2, the second agency code number (corresponding to letter Q) should be "9," not "8." Column 3 is coded correctly to Column 1. Since there is an error only in Column 2, the correct answer is A.

	Column 1	Column 2	Column 3	
1.	QLNRCA	931268	ifegnd	1.____
2.	NRMOTC	127546	egftbn	2.____
3.	RCTALM	265837	gndbrt	3.____
4.	TAMLON	578341	bdtrfe	4.____
5.	ANTROM	815427	debigt	5.____
6.	MRALON	728341	tgdrfe	6.____
7.	CTNQRO	657924	ndeigf	7.____
8.	QMROTA	972458	itgfbd	8.____

	Column 1	Column 2	Column 3	
9.	RQMCOL	297463	gitnfr	9.____
10.	NOMRTQ	147259	eftgbi	10.____

KEY (CORRECT ANSWERS)

1.	D	6.	D
2.	C	7.	C
3.	B	8.	D
4.	A	9.	A
5.	B	10.	D

TEST 6

DIRECTIONS: Each of Questions 1 through 6 consist of three lines of code letters and numbers. The numbers on each line should correspond to the code letter on the same line in accordance with the table below.

Code Letter:	D	Y	K	L	P	U	S	R	A	E
Corresponding Number:	0	1	2	3	4	5	6	7	8	9

On some of the lines an error exists in the coding. Prepare the letters and numbers in each question carefully. If you find an error or errors on

only one of the lines in the question, mark your answer A;
any two lines in the question, mark your answer B;
all three lines in the question, mark your answer C;
none of the lines in the question, mark your answer D.

SAMPLE QUESTION

KSRYELD 2671930
SAPUEKL 6845913
RYKADLP 5128034

In the above sample, the first line is correct since each code letter listed has the correct corresponding number. On the second line, an error exists because code letter R should have the number 2 instead of number 1. On the third line, an error exists because the code letter R should have the number 7 instead of the number 5. Since there are errors on two of the three lines, the correct answer is B.

Now answer the following questions using the same procedure.

1. YPUSRLD 1456730 1.____
UPSAEDY 5648901
PREYDKS 4791026

2. AERLPUS 8973456 2.____
DKLYDPA 0231048
UKLDREP 5230794

3. DAPUSLA 0845683 3.____
YKLDLPS 1230356
PUSKYDE 4562101

4. LRPUPDL 3745403 4.____
SUPLEDR 6543907
PKEYDLU 4291025

5. KEYDESR 2910967 5.____
PRSALEY 4678391
LRAYSK 3687162

6.	YESREYL	1967913	6.____
	PLPRAKY	4346821	
	YLPSRDU	1346705	

KEY (CORRECT ANSWERS)

1.	A	4.	A
2.	D	5.	B
3.	C	6.	A

ARITHMETICAL REASONING
EXAMINATION SECTION
TEST 1

DIRECTIONS: Each question or incomplete statement is followed by several suggested answers or completions. Select the one that BEST answers the question or completes the statement. *PRINT THE LETTER OF THE CORRECT ANSWER IN THE SPACE AT THE RIGHT.*

1. If a secretary answered 28 phone calls and typed the addresses for 112 credit statements in one morning, what is the RATIO of phone calls answered to credit statements typed for that period of time? 1.____

   A. 1:4 B. 1:7 C. 2:3 D. 3:5

2. According to a suggested filing system, no more than 10 folders should be filed behind any one file guide and from 15 to 25 file guides should be used in each file drawer for easy finding and filing. 2.____
   The MAXIMUM number of folders that a five-drawer file cabinet can hold to allow easy finding and filing is

   A. 550 B. 750 C. 1,100 D. 1,250

3. An employee had a starting salary of $19,353. He received a salary increase at the end of each year, and at the end of the seventh year his salary was $25,107. 3.____
   What was his AVERAGE annual increase in salary over these seven years?

   A. $765 B. $807 C. $822 D. $858

4. The 55 typists and 28 senior clerks in a certain agency were paid a total of $1,457,400 in salaries in 2005. 4.____
   If the average annual salary of a typist was $16,800, the average annual salary of a senior clerk was

   A. $19,050 B. $19,950 C. $20,100 D. $20,250

5. A typist has been given a three-page report to type. She has finished typing the first two pages. The first page has 283 words, and the second page has 366 words. 5.____
   If the total report consists of 954 words, how many words will she have to type on the third page of the report?

   A. 202 B. 287 C. 305 D. 313

6. In one day, Clerk A processed 30% more forms than Clerk B, and Clerk C processed 1 1/4 as many forms as Clerk A. 6.____
   If Clerk B processed 40 forms, how many more forms were processed by Clerk C than Clerk B?

   A. 12 B. 13 C. 21 D. 25

7. A clerk who earns a gross salary of $678 every 2 weeks has the following deductions taken from her paycheck: 15% for city, state, and federal taxes; 2 1/2% for Social Security; $1.95 for health insurance; and $9.00 for union dues. 7.____
The amount of her take-home pay is

A. $429.60 B. $468.60 C. $497.40 D. $548.40

8. In 2002, an agency spent $400 to buy pencils at a cost of $1.00 a dozen. 8.____
If the agency used 3/4 of these pencils in 2002 and used the same number of pencils in 2003, how many more pencils did it have to buy to have enough pencils for all of 2003?

A. 1,200 B. 2,400 C. 3,600 D. 4,800

9. A clerk who worked in Agency X earned the following salaries: $15,105 the first year, $15,750 the second year, and $16,440 the third year. Another clerk who worked in Agency Y for three years earned $15,825 a year for two years and $16,086 the third year. 9.____
The DIFFERENCE between the average salaries received by both clerks over a three-year period is

A. $147 B. $153 C. $261 D. $423

10. An employee who works more than 40 hours in any week receives overtime payment for the extra hours at time and one-half (1 1/2 times) his hourly rate of pay. An employee who earns $13.60 an hour works a total of 45 hours during a certain week. 10.____
His TOTAL pay for that week would be

A. $564.40 B. $612.00 C. $646.00 D. $824.00

11. Suppose that the amount of money spent for supplies in 2006 for a division in a city department was $156,500. This represented an increase of 12% over the amount spent for supplies for this division in 2005. 11.____
The amount of money spent for supplies for this division in 2005 was MOST NEARLY

A. $139,730 B. $137,720 C. $143,460 D. $138,720

12. Suppose that a group of five clerks have been assigned to insert 24,000 letters into envelopes. The clerks perform this work at the following rates of speed: Clerk A, 1,100 letters an hour; Clerk B, 1,450 letters an hour; Clerk C, 1,200 letters an hour; Clerk D, 1,300 letters an hour; Clerk E, 1,250 letters an hour. At the end of two hours of work, Clerks C and D are assigned to another task. 12.____
From the time that Clerks C and D were taken off the assignment, the number of hours required for the remaining clerks to complete this assignment is

A. less than 3 hours
B. 3 hours
C. more than 3 hours, but less than 4 hours
D. more than 4 hours

13. The number 60 is 40% of 13.____

A. 24 B. 84 C. 96 D. 150

14. If 3/8 of a number is 96, the number is 14.____

A. 132 B. 36 C. 256 D. 156

15. A city department uses an average of 25 20-cent, 35 30-cent, and 350 40-cent postage stamps each day. 15.____
The TOTAL cost of stamps used by the department in a five-day period is

A. $29.50 B. $155.50 C. $290.50 D. $777.50

16. A city department issued 12,000 applications in 2000. The number of applications that the department issued in 1998 was 25% greater than the number it issued in 2000. 16.____
If the department issued 10% fewer applications in 1996 than it did in 1998, the number it issued in 1996 was

A. 16,500 B. 13,500 C. 9,900 D. 8,100

17. A clerk can add 40 columns of figures an hour by using an adding machine and 20 columns of figures an hour without using an adding machine. 17.____
The TOTAL number of hours it would take him to add 200 columns if he does 3/5 of the work by machine and the rest without the machine is

A. 6 B. 7 C. 8 D. 9

18. In 1997, a city department bought 500 dozen pencils at $1.20 per dozen. In 2000, only 75 percent as many pencils were bought as were bought in 1997, but the price was 20 percent higher than the 1997 price. The TOTAL cost of the pencils bought in 2000 was 18.____

A. $540 B. $562.50 C. $720 D. $750

19. A clerk is assigned to check the accuracy of the entries on 490 forms. He checks 40 forms an hour. After working one hour on this task, he is joined by another clerk, who checks these forms at the rate of 35 an hour. 19.____
The TOTAL number of hours required to do the entire assignment is

A. 5 B. 6 C. 7 D. 8

20. Assume that there are a total of 420 employees in a city agency. Thirty percent of the employees are clerks, and 1/7 are typists. 20.____
The DIFFERENCE between the number of clerks and the number of typists is

A. 126 B. 66 C. 186 D. 80

21. Assume that a duplicating machine produces copies of a bulletin at a cost of 2 cents per copy. The machine produces 120 copies of the bulletin per minute. 21.____
If the cost of producing a certain number of copies was $12, how many minutes of operation did it take the machine to produce this number of copies?

A. 5 B. 2 C. 10 D. 6

22. An assignment is completed by 32 clerks in 22 days. Assuming that all the clerks work at the same rate of speed, the number of clerks that would be needed to complete this assignment in 16 days is 22.____

A. 27 B. 38 C. 44 D. 52

23. A department head hired a total of 60 temporary employees to handle a seasonal increase in the department's workload. The following lists the number of temporary employees hired, their rates of pay, and the duration of their employment: 23.____
    One-third of the total were hired as clerks, each at the rate of $27,500 a year, for two months.
    30 percent of the total were hired as office machine operators, each at the rate of $31,500 a year, for four months.
    22 stenographers were hired, each at the rate of $30,000 a year, for three months.
    The total amount paid to these temporary employees was MOST NEARLY

    A. $1,780,000 B. $450,000
    C. $650,000 D. $390,000

24. Assume that there are 2,300 employees in a city agency. Also, assume that five percent of these employees are accountants, that 80 percent of the accountants have college degrees, and that one-half of the accountants who have college degrees have five years of experience. Then, the number of employees in the agency who are accountants with college degrees and five years of experience is 24.____

    A. 46 B. 51 C. 460 D. 920

25. Assume that the regular 8-hour working day of a laborer is from 8 A.M. to 5 P.M., with an hour off for lunch. He earns a regular hourly rate of pay for these 8 hours and is paid at the rate of time-and-a-half for each hour worked after his regular working day. 25.____
    If, on a certain day, he works from 8 A.M. to 6 P.M., with an hour off for lunch, and earns $171, his regular hourly rate of pay is

    A. $16.30 B. $17.10 C. $18.00 D. $19.00

KEY (CORRECT ANSWERS)

1. A
2. D
3. C
4. A
5. C

6. D
7. D
8. B
9. A
10. C

11. A
12. B
13. D
14. C
15. D

16. B
17. B
18. A
19. C
20. B

21. A
22. C
23. B
24. A
25. C

SOLUTIONS TO PROBLEMS

1. 28/112 is equivalent to 1:4
2. Maximum number of folders = (10)(25)(5) = 1250
3. Average annual increase = ($25,107-19,353) ÷ 7 = $822
4. $1,457,400 - (55)($16,800) = $533,400 = total amount paid to senior clerks. Average senior clerk's salary = $533,400 ÷ 28 = $19,050
5. Number of words on 3rd page = 954 - 283 - 366 = 305
6. Clerk A processed (40)(1.30) = 52 forms and clerk C processed (52)(1.25) = 65 forms. Finally, 65 - 40 = 25
7. Take-home pay = $678 - (.15)($678) - (.025)($678) - $1.95 - $9.00 = $548.40
8. (400)(12) = 4800 pencils. In 2002, (3/4)(4800) = 3600 were used, so that 1200 pencils were available at the beginning of 2003. Since 3600 pencils were also used in 2003, the agency had to buy 3600 - 1200 = 2400 pencils.
9. Average salary for clerk in Agency X = ($15,105+$15,750+$16,440)/3 = $15,765. Average salary for clerk in Agency Y = ($15,825+ $15,825+$16,086) ÷ 3 = $15,912. Difference in average salaries = $147.
10. Total pay = ($13.60)(40) + ($20.40)(5) = $646.00
11. In 2005, amount spent = $156,500 ÷ 1.12 ≈ $139,730 (Actual value = $139,732.1429)
12. At the end of 2 hours, (1100)(2) + (1450)(2) + (1200)(2) + (1300X2) + (1250X2) = 12,600 letters have been inserted into envelopes. The remaining 11,400 letters done by clerks A, B, and C will require 11,400 ÷ (1100+1450+1250) = 3 hours.
13. 60 ÷ .40 = 150
14. 96 ÷ 3/8 = (96)(8/3) = 256
15. Total cost = (5)[(25)(.20)+(35)(.30)+(350)(.40)]= $777.50
16. In 1998, (12,000) (1.25) = 15,000 applications were issued In 1996, (15,000)(.90) = 13,500 applications were issued
17. Total number of hours $= \frac{120}{40} + \frac{80}{20} = 7$
18. (.75)(500 dozen) = 375 dozen purchased in 2000 at a cost of ($1.20)(1.20) = $1.44 per dozen. Total cost for 2000 = ($1.44) (375) = $540
19. Total time = 1 hour + 450/75 hrs. = 7 hours
20. (.30)(420) - (1/7)(420) = 126 - 60 = 66

21. Cost per minute = (120)(.02) = \$2.40. Then, \$12 ÷ \$2.40 = 5 minutes

22. (32)(22) ÷ 16 = 44 clerks

23. Total amount paid = (20)(\$27,500)(2/12) + (18)(\$31,500) (4/12) + (22)(\$30,000)(3/12) = \$445,666.$\overline{6}$ ≈ \$450,000

24. Number of accountants with college degrees and five years of experience = (2300)(.05)(.80)(1/2) = 46

25. Let x = regular hourly pay. Then, (8)(x) + (1)(1.5x) = \$1.71 So, 9.5x = 171. Solving, x = \$18

TEST 2

DIRECTIONS: Each question or incomplete statement is followed by several suggested answers or completions. Select the one that BEST answers the question or completes the statement. *PRINT THE LETTER OF THE CORRECT ANSWER IN THE SPACE AT THE RIGHT.*

1. Assume that you know the capacity of a filing cabinet, the extent of which it is filled, and the daily rate at which material is being added to the file. 1.____
In order to estimate how many more days it will take for the cabinet to be filled to capacity, you should

   A. divide the extent to which the cabinet is filled by the daily rate
   B. take the difference between the capacity of the cabinet and the material in it, and multiply the result by the daily rate of adding material
   C. divide the daily rate of adding material by the difference between the capacity of the cabinet and the material in it
   D. take the difference between the capacity of the cabinet and the material in it, and divide the result by the daily rate of adding material

2. Suppose you have been asked to compute the average salary earned in your department during the past year. For each of the divisions of the department, you are given the number of employees and the average salary. 2.____
In order to find the requested overall average salary for the department, you should

   A. add the average salaries of the various divisions and divide the total by the number of divisions
   B. multiply the number of employees in each division by the corresponding average salary, add the results and divide the total by the number of employees in the department
   C. add the average salaries of the various divisions and divide the total by the total number of employees in the department
   D. multiply the sum of the average salaries of the various divisions by the total number of divisions and divide the resulting product by the total number of employees in the department

3. Suppose that a group of six clerks has been assigned to assemble the duplicated pages of a report into completed copies. After four hours of work, they have been able to complete one-third of the job. 3.____
In order to assemble all the remaining copies in three more hours of work, the number of clerks which will have to be added to the original six, assuming that all the clerks assigned to this task work at the same rate of speed, is

   A. 10 B. 16 C. 2 D. 6

4. A study of the grades of students in a certain college revealed that in 2005, 15% fewer students received a passing grade in mathematics than in 2004, whereas in 2006 the number of students passing mathematics increased 15% over 2005. 4.____
On the basis of this study, it would be MOST accurate to conclude that

   A. the same percentage of students passed mathematics in 2004 as in 2006
   B. of the three years studied, the greatest percentage of students passed mathematics in 2006

C. the percentage of students who passed mathematics in 2006 was less than the percentage passing this subject in 2004
D. the percentage of students passing mathematics in 2004 was 15% greater than the percentage of students passing this subject in 2006

5. A city department employs 1,400 people, of whom 35% are clerks and 1/8 are stenographers. 5.___
The number of employees in the department who are neither clerks nor stenographers is

A. 640 B. 665 C. 735 D. 760

6. Assume that there are 190 papers to be filed and that Clerk A and Clerk B are assigned to file these papers. If Clerk A files 40 papers more than Clerk B, then the number of papers that Clerk A files is 6.___

A. 75 B. 110 C. 115 D. 150

7. A stock clerk had on hand the following items: 7.___
500 pads, each worth 16 cents
130 pencils, each worth 12 cents
50 dozen rubber bands, worth 8 cents a dozen
If, from this stock, he issued 125 pads, 45 pencils, and 48 rubber bands, the value of the remaining stock would be

A. $25.72 B. $27.80 C. $70.52 D. $73.88

8. In a particular agency, there were 160 accidents in 2002. Of these accidents, 75% were due to unsafe acts and the rest were due to unsafe conditions. In the following year, a special safety program was established. The number of accidents in 2004 due to unsafe acts was reduced to 35% of what it had been in 2002. 8.___
How many accidents due to unsafe acts were there in 2004?

A. 20 B. 36 C. 42 D. 56

9. At the end of every month, the petty cash fund of Agency A is reimbursed for payments made from the fund during the month. During the month of February, the amounts paid from the fund were entered on receipts as follows: 10 bus fares of $1.40 each and one taxi fare of $14.00. At the end of the month, the money left in the fund was in the following denominations: 60 one-dollar bills, 16 quarters, 40 dimes, and 80 nickels. 9.___
If the petty cash fund is reduced by 20% for the following month, how much money will there be available in the petty cash fund for March?

A. $44 B. $80 C. $86 D. $100

10. An employee worked on a job for 6 weeks, 5 days per week, and 8 hours per day. 10.___
How many hours did he work on the job?

A. 40 B. 48 C. 55 D. 240

11. Divide 35 by .7. 11.___

A. 5 B. 42 C. 50 D. 245

12. .1% of 25 = 12.____

A. .025 B. .25 C. 2.5 D. 25

13. In a city agency, 80 percent of the total number of employees are more than 25 years of age and 65 percent of the total number of employees are high school graduates. 13.____
The SMALLEST possible percent of employees who are both high school graduates and more than 25 years of age is

A. 35% B. 45% C. 55% D. 65%

14. Two clerical units, X and Y, each having a different number of clerks, are assigned to file registration cards. It takes Unit X, which contains 8 clerks, 21 days to file the same number of cards that Unit Y can file in 28 days. It is also a fact that Unit X can file 174,528 cards in 72 days. 14.____
Assuming that all the clerks in both units work at the same rate of speed, the number of cards which can be filed by Unit Y in 144 days, if 4 more clerks are added to the staff of Unit Y, is MOST NEARLY

A. 392,000 B. 436,000 C. 523,000 D. 669,000

15. Assume that two machines, each costing $14,750, were purchased for your office. Each machine requires the services of an operator at a salary of $2,000 per month. These machines are to replace six clerks, two of whom earn $1,550 per month each, and four of whom earn $1,700 per month each. 15.____
The number of months it will take for the cost of the machines to be made up from the savings in salaries is

A. less than four
B. four
C. five
D. more than five

16. Suppose that the amount of stationery used by your department in August decreased by 16% as compared with the amount used in July, and that the amount used in September increased by 25% as compared with the amount used in August. 16.____
The amount of stationery used in September as compared with the amount used in July is

A. greater by 5 percent
B. less by 5 percent
C. greater by 9 percent
D. the same

17. An employee earns $48 a day and works 5 days a week. 17.____
He will earn $2,160 in _______ weeks.

A. 5 B. 7 C. 8 D. 9

18. In a certain bureau, the entire staff consists of 1 senior supervisor, 2 supervisors, 6 assistant supervisors, and 54 associate workers. 18.____
The percent of the staff who are not associate workers is MOST NEARLY

A. 14 B. 21 C. 27 D. 32

19. In a certain bureau, five employees each earn $1,000 a month, another 3 employees each earn $2,200 a month, and another two employees each earn $1,400 a month. 19.____
The monthly payroll for these employees is

A. $3,600 B. $8,800 C. $11,400 D. $14,400

20. An employee contributes 5% of his salary to the pension fund. 20.______
If his salary is $1,200 a month, the amount of his contribution to the pension fund in a year is

A. $480 B. $720 C. $960 D. $1,200

21. The number of square feet in an area that is 50 feet long and 30 feet wide is 21.______

A. 80 B. 150 C. 800 D. 1,500

22. A farm hand was paid a weekly wage of $332.16 for a 48-hour work week. As a result of a new labor contract, he is paid $344.96 a week for a 44-hour work week with time and one-half pay for time worked in excess of 44 hours in any work week. 22.______
If he continues to work 48 hours weekly under the new contract, the amount by which his average hourly rate for a 48-hour work week under the new contract exceeds the hourly rate previously paid him lies between _______ and _______ cents, inclusive.

A. 91;100 B. 101;110 C. 111;120 D. 121;130

23. Each side of a square room, which is being used as an office, measures 66 feet. The floor of the room is divided by six traffic aisles, each aisle being six feet wide. Three of the aisles run parallel to the east and west sides of the room, and the other three run parallel to the north and south sides of the room, so that the remaining floor space is divided into 16 equal sections. If all of the floor space which is not being used for traffic aisles is occupied by desk and chair sets, and each set takes up 24 square feet of floor space, the number of desk and chair sets in the room is 23.______

A. 80 B. 64 C. 36 D. 96

24. In 2005, a city agency bought 12,000 envelopes at $4.00 per hundred. In 2006, the price of envelopes purchased was 40 percent higher than the 2005 price, but only 60 percent as many envelopes were bought. 24.______
The total cost of the envelopes purchased in 2006 was MOST NEARLY

A. $250 B. $320 C. $400 D. $480

25. In a city agency, 25 percent of the women employees and 50 percent of the men employees attended a general staff meeting. 25.______
If 48 percent of all the employees in the agency are women, the percentage of all the employees who attended the meeting is

A. 36% B. 37% C. 38% D. 75%

KEY (CORRECT ANSWERS)

1. D
2. B
3. A
4. C
5. C
6. C
7. D
8. C
9. B
10. D
11. C
12. A
13. B
14. A
15. C
16. A
17. D
18. A
19. D
20. B
21. D
22. D
23. D
24. C
25. C

SOLUTIONS TO PROBLEMS

1. To determine number of days required to fill cabinet to capacity, subtract material in it from capacity amount, then divide by daily rate of adding material. Example: A cabinet already has 10 folders in it, and the capacity is 100 folders. Suppose 5 folders per day are added. Number of days to fill to capacity = (100-10) ÷ 5 = 18

2. To determine overall average salary, multiply number of employees in each division by that division's average salary, add results, then divide by total number of employees. Example: Division A has 4 employees with average salary of $40,000; division B has 6 employees with average salary of $36,000; division C has 2 employees with average salary of $46,000. Average salary = [(4)($40,000)+(6)($36,000)+(2)($46,000)] / 12 = $39,000

3. (6)(4) = 24 clerk-hours. Since only one-third of work has been done, (24) (3) - 24 = 48 clerk-hours remain. Then, 48 3 = 16 clerks. Thus, 16 - 6 = 10 additional clerks.

4. The percentage of students passing math in 2006 was less than the percentage of those passing math in 2004. Example: Suppose 400 students passed math in 2004. Then, (400)(.85) = 340 passed in 2005. Finally, (340)(1.15) = 391 passed in 2006.

5. 1400 - (.35)(1400) - (1/8)(1400) = 735

6. Let x = number of papers filed by clerk A, x-40 = number of papers filed by clerk B. Then, x + (x-40) = 190 Solving, x = 115

7. (500-125)(.16) + (130-45)(.12) + (50 - 48/12)(.08) = $60.00 + $10.20 + $3.68 = $73.88

8. (160)(.75) = 120 accidents due to unsafe acts in 2002. In 2004, (120)(.35) = 42 accidents due to unsafe acts

9. Original amount at beginning of February in the fund = (10)($1.40) + (1)($14.00) + (60)($1) + (16)(.25) + (40)(.10) + (80)(.05) = $100. Finally, for March, ($100)(.80) = $80 will be available

10. Total hours = (6)(5)(8) = 240

11. 35 ÷ .7 = 50

12. .1% of 25 = (.001)(25) = .025

13. Let A = percent of employees who are at least 25 years old and B = percent of employees who are high school graduates. Also, let N = percent of employees who fit neither category and J = percent of employees who are in both categories.
    Then, 100 = A + B + N - J. Substituting, 100 = 80 + 65 + N - J To minimize J, let N = 0. So, 100 = 80 + 65 + 0 - J. Solving, J = 45

14. Let Y = number of clerks in Unit Y. Then, (8)(21) = (4)(28), so Y = 6. Unit X has 8 clerks who can file 174,528 cards in 72 flays; thus, each clerk in Unit X can file 174,528 ÷ 72 ÷ 8 = 303 cards per day. Adding 4 clerks to Unit Y will yield 10 clerks in that unit. Since their rate is equal to that of Unit X, the clerks in Unit Y will file, in 144 days, is (303)(10)(144) = 436,320 ≈ 436,000 cards.

15. Let x = required number of months. The cost of the machines in x months = (2)(14,750) + (2)(2000)(x) = 29,500 + 4000x. The savings in salaries for the displaced clerks = x[(2)(1550) +(4)(1700)] = 9900x. Thus, 29,500 + 4000x = 9900x. Solving, x = 5. So, five months will elapse in order to achieve a savings in cost.

16. Let x = amount used in July, so that .84x = amount used in August. For September, the amount used = (.84x)(1.25) = 1.05x. This means the amount used in September is 5% more than the amount used in July.

17. Each week he earns ($48)(5) = $240. Then, $2160 ÷ $240 = 9 weeks

18. (1+2+6) ÷ 63 = 1/7 ≈ 14%

19. Monthly payroll = (5)($1000) + (3)($2200) + (2)($1400) = $14,400

20. Yearly contribution to pension fund = (12)($1200)(.05) = $720

21. (50')(30') = 1500 sq.ft.

22. Old rate = 332.16 ÷ 48 = 6.92 (48 hours)
New rate = 344.96 (44 hours)
Overtime rate = 344.96 ÷ 44 = 7.75/hr. x 1.5 x 4 = 46.48
344.96 + 46.48 = 391.44
391.44 ÷ 48 = 8.15
815 - 692 = 123 cents an hour more

23. Each of the 16 sections is a square with side [66'-(3)(6')] ÷ 4 = 12'. So each section contains (12')(12') = 144 sq.ft.
The number of desk and chair sets = (144 ÷ 24) (16) = 96

24. In 2006, (.60)(12,000) = 7200 envelopes were bought and the price per hundred was ($4.00)(1.40) = $5.60. The total cost = (5.60)(72) = $403.20 ≈ $400

25. (.25)(.48) + (.50)(.52) = .38 = 38%

TEST 3

DIRECTIONS: Each question or incomplete statement is followed by several suggested answers or completions. Select the one that BEST answers the question or completes the statement. *PRINT THE LETTER OF THE CORRECT ANSWER IN THE SPACE AT THE RIGHT.*

1. According to one suggested filing system, no more than 12 folders should be filed behind any one file guide and from 10 to 20 file guides should be used in each file drawer. Based on this filing system, the MAXIMUM number of folders that a four-drawer file cabinet can hold is 1.____

   A. 240 B. 480 C. 960 D. 1,200

2. A certain office uses three different forms. Last year, it used 3,500 copies of Form L, 6,700 copies of Form M, and 10,500 copies of Form P. This year, the office expects to decrease the use of each of these forms by 5%. The TOTAL number of these three forms which the office expects to use this year is 2.____

   A. 10,350 B. 16,560 C. 19,665 D. 21,735

3. The hourly rate of pay for a certain part-time employee is computed by dividing his yearly salary rate by the number of hours in the work year. The employee's yearly salary rate is $18,928, and there are 1,820 hours in the work year.
   If this employee works 18 hours during one week, his TOTAL earnings for these 18 hours are 3.____

   A. $180.00 B. $183.60 C. $187.20 D. $190.80

4. Assume that the regular work week of an employee is 35 hours and that the employee is paid for any extra hours worked according to the following schedule. For hours worked in excess of 35 hours, up to and including 40 hours, the employee receives his regular hourly rate of pay. For hours worked in excess of 40 hours, the employee receives 1 1/2 times his hourly rate of pay.
   If the employee's hourly rate of pay is $11.20 and he works 43 hours during a certain week, his TOTAL pay for the week would be 4.____

   A. $481.60 B. $498.40 C. $556.00 D. $722.40

5. A clerk divided his 35 hour work week as follows: 5.____
   1/5 of his time in sorting mail;
   1/2 of his time in filing letters; and
   1/7 of his time in reception work.
   The rest of his time was devoted to messenger work. The percentage of time spent on messenger work by the clerk during the week was MOST NEARLY

   A. 6% B. 10% C. 14% D. 16%

6. A city department has set up a computing unit and has rented 5 computing machines at a yearly rental of $700 per machine. In addition, the cost to the department for the maintenance and repair of each of these machines is $50 per year. Five computing machine operators, each receiving an annual salary of $15,000, and a supervisor, who receives $19,000 a year, have been assigned to this unit. This unit will perform the work previously performed by 10 employees whose combined salary was $162,000 a year.
   On the basis of these facts, the savings that will result from the operation of this computing unit for 5 years will be MOST NEARLY 6.____

   A. $250,000 B. $320,000 C. $330,000 D. $475,000

7. Twelve clerks are assigned to enter certain data on index cards. This number of clerks could perform the task in 18 days. After these clerks have worked on this assignment for 6 days, 4 more clerks are added to the staff to do this work. 7.____
Assuming that all the clerks work at the same rate of speed, the entire task, instead of taking 18 days, will be performed in ______ days.

A. 9 B. 12 C. 15 D. 16

8. Suppose that a file cabinet, which has a capacity of 3,000 cards, now contains approximately 2,200 cards. Cards are added to the file at the average rate of 30 cards a day. 8.____
To find the number of days it will take to fill the cabinet to capacity,

A. divide 3,000 by 30
B. divide 2,200 by 3,000
C. divide 800 by 30
D. multiply 30 by the fraction 2,200 divided by 3,000

9. Six gross of special drawing pencils were purchased for use in a city department. 9.____
If the pencils were used at the rate of 24 a week, the MAXIMUM number of weeks that the six gross of pencils would last is ______ weeks.

A. 6 B. 12 C. 24 D. 36

10. A stock clerk had 600 pads on hand. He then issued 3/8 of his supply of pads to Division X, 1/4 to Division Y, and 1/6 to Division Z. 10.____
The number of pads remaining in stock is

A. 48 B. 125 C. 240 D. 475

11. If a certain job can be performed by 18 clerks in 26 days, the number of clerks needed to perform the job in 12 days is ______ clerks. 11.____

A. 24 B. 30 C. 39 D. 52

12. In anticipation of a seasonal increase in the amount of work to be performed by his division, a division chief prepared the following list of additional temporary employees needed by his division and the amount of time they would be employed: 12.____
26 cashiers, each at $24,000 a year, for 2 months
15 laborers, each at $85.00 a day, for 50 days
6 clerks, each at $21,000 a year, for 3 months
The total approximate cost for this additional personnel would be MOST NEARLY

A. $200,000 B. $250,000 C. $500,000 D. $600,000

13. A copy machine company offered to sell a city agency 4 copy machines at a discount of 15% from the list price, and to allow the agency $850 for each of its two old machines. 13.____
The list price of the new machines is $6,250 per machine.
If the city agency accepts this offer, the amount of money it will have to provide for the purchase of these 4 machines is

A. $17,350 B. $22,950 C. $19,550 D. $18,360

14. A stationery buyer was offered bond paper at the following price scale: 14.___
    $1.43 per ream for the first 1,000 reams
    $1.30 per ream for the next 4,000 reams
    $1.20 per ream for each additional ream beyond 5,000 reams
    If the buyer ordered 10,000 reams of paper, the average cost per ream, computed to the nearest cent, was

    A. $1.24 B. $1.26 C. $1.31 D. $1.36

15. A clerk has 5.70 percent of his salary deducted for his retirement pension. 15.___
    If this clerk's annual salary is $20,400, the monthly deduction for his retirement pension is

    A. $298.20 B. $357.90 C. $1,162.80 D. $96.90

16. In a certain bureau, two-thirds of the employees are clerks and the remainder are typists. 16.___
    If there are 90 clerks, then the number of typists in this bureau is

    A. 135 B. 45 C. 120 D. 30

17. The number of investigations conducted by an agency in 1999 was 3,600. In 2000, the number of investigations conducted was one-third more than in 1999. The number of investigations conducted in 2001 was three-fourths of the number conducted in 2000. It is anticipated that the number of investigations conducted in 2002 will be equal to the average of the three preceding years. On the basis of this information, the MOST accurate of the following statements is that the number of investigations conducted in 17.___

    A. 1999 is larger than the number anticipated for 2002
    B. 2000 is smaller than the number anticipated for 2002
    C. 2001 is equal to the number conducted in 1999
    D. 2001 is larger than the number anticipated in 2002

18. A city agency engaged in repair work uses a small part which the city purchases for 14 each. Assume that, in a certain year, the total expenditure of the city for this part was $700. 18.___
    How many of these parts were purchased that year?

    A. 50 B. 200 C. 2,000 D. 5,000

19. The work unit which you supervise is responsible for processing 15 reports per month. If your unit has 4 clerks and the best worker completes 40% of the reports himself, how many reports would each of the other clerks have to complete if they all do an equal number? 19.___

    A. 1 B. 2 C. 3 D. 4

20. Assume that the work unit in which you work has 24 clerks and 18 stenographers. In order to change the ratio of stenographers to clerks so that there is 1 stenographer for every 4 clerks, it would be necessary to REDUCE the number of stenographers by 20.____

A. 3 B. 6 C. 9 D. 12

21. The arithmetic mean salary for five employees earning $18,500, $18,300, $18,600, $18,400, and $18,500, respectively, is 21.____

A. $18,450 B. $18,460 C. $18,475 D. $18,500

22. Last year, a city department which is responsible for purchasing supplies ordered bond paper in equal quantities from 22 different companies. The price was exactly the same for each company, and the total cost for the 22 orders was $693,113. Assuming prices did not change during the year, the cost of each order was MOST NEARLY 22.____

A. $31,490 B. $31,495 C. $31,500 D. $31,505

23. Suppose that a large bureau has 187 employees. On a particular day, approximately 14% of these employees are not available for work because of absences due to vacation, illness, or other reasons. Of the remaining employees, 1/7 are assigned to a special project while the balance are assigned to the normal work of the bureau. The number of employees assigned to the normal work of the bureau on that day is 23.____

A. 112 B. 124 C. 138 D. 142

24. Suppose that you are in charge of a typing pool of 8 typists. Two typists type at the rate of 38 words per minute; three type at the rate of 40 words per minute; three type at the rate of 42 words per minute. The average typewritten page consists of 50 lines, 12 words per line. Each employee works from 9 to 5 with one hour off for lunch. The total number of pages typed by this pool in one day is, on the average, CLOSEST to ______ pages. 24.____

A. 205 B. 225 C. 250 D. 275

25. Suppose that part-time workers are paid $7.20 an hour, prorated to the nearest half hour, with pay guaranteed for a minimum of four hours if services are required for less than four hours. In one operation, part-time workers signed the time sheet as follows: 25.____

Worker	In	Out
A	8:00 A.M.	11:35 A.M.
B	8:30 A.M.	3:20 P.M.
C	7:55 A.M.	11:00 A.M.
D	8:30 A.M.	2:25 P.M.

How much would TOTAL payment to these part-time workers amount to for this operation, assuming that those who stayed after 12 Noon were not paid for one hour which they took off for lunch?

A. $134.40 B. $136.80 C. $142.20 D. $148.80

KEY (CORRECT ANSWERS)

1. C
2. C
3. C
4. B
5. D
6. B
7. C
8. C
9. D
10. B
11. C
12. A
13. C
14. B
15. D
16. B
17. C
18. D
19. C
20. D
21. B
22. D
23. C
24. B
25. B

SOLUTIONS TO PROBLEMS

1. Maximum number of folders = (4)(12)(20) = 960

2. (3500+6700+10,500)(.95) = 19,665

3. Hourly rate = $18,928 ÷ 1820 = $10.40. Then, the pay for 18 hours = ($10.40)(18) = $187.20

4. Total pay = ($11.20)(40) + ($11.20)(1.5)(3) = $498.40

5. (1 - 1/5 - 1/2 - 1/7)(100)% ≈ 16%

6. Previous cost for five years = ($324,000)(5) = $1,620,000
   Present cost for five years = (5)(5)($1,400) + (5)(5)($100) + (5)(5)($30,000) + (1)(5)($38,000) = $977,500 The net savings = $642,500 ≈ $640,000

7. (12)(18) = 216 clerk-days. Then, 216 - (12)(6) = 144 clerk-days of work left when 4 more clerks are added. Now, 16 clerks will finish the task in 144 ÷ 16 = 9 more days. Finally, the task will require a total of 6 + 9 = 15 days.

8. Number of days needed = (3000-2200) ÷ 30 = 26.7, which is equivalent to dividing 800 by 30.

9. (6)(144) = 864 pencils purchased. Then, 864 ÷ 24 = 36 maximum number of weeks

10. Number of remaining pads = 600 - (1)(600) - (1/4)(600) - (1/6)(600) = 125

11. (18)(26) ÷ 12 = 39 clerks

12. Total cost = (26)($24,000)(2/12) + (15)($85)(50) + (6)($21,000)(3/12) = $199,250 $200,000

13. (4)($6250)(.85) - (2)($850) = $19,550

14. Total cost = ($1.43)(1000) + ($1.30)(4000) + ($1.20X5000) = $12,630. Average cost per ream = $12,630 10,000 ≈ $1.26

15. Monthly salary = $20,400 ÷ 12 = $1700. Thus, the monthly deduction for his pension = ($1700)(.057) + $96.90

16. Number of employees = 90 ÷ 2/3 = 135. Then, the number of typists = (1/3)(135) = 45

17. The number of investigations for each year is as follows:
    1999: 3600
    2000: (3600)(1 1/3) = 4800
    2001: (4800)(3/4) = 3600
    2002: (3600+4800+3600)/3 = 4000
    So, the number of investigations were equal for 1999 and 2001.

18. $700 ÷ .14 = 5000 parts

19. The best worker does (.40)(15) = 6 reports. The other 9 reports are divided equally among the other 3 clerks, so each clerk does 9 $\div$ 3 = 3 reports.

20. 1:4 = 6:24 . Thus, the number of stenographers must be reduced by 18 - 6 = 12

21. Mean = ($18,500+$18,300+$18,400+$18,500) $\div$ 5 = $18,460

22. The cost per order = $693,113 $\div$ 22 $\approx$ $31,505

23. 187 - (.14) = 26. 187 - 26 = 161 - 1/7 (161) = 23
161 - 23 = 138

24. Number of words typed in 1 min. = (2)(38) + (3)(40) + (3)(42) = 322. For 7 hours, the total number of words typed = (7)(60)(322) = 135,240. Each page contains (on the average) (50)(12) = 600 words. Finally, 135,240 $\div$ 600 $\approx$ 225 pages

25. Worker A = ($7.20)(4) = $28.80
Worker B = ($7.20)(3 1/2) + ($7.20)(2 1/2) = $43.20
Worker C = ($7.20)(4) = $28.80
Worker D = ($7.20)(3 1/2) + ($7.20)(1 1/2) = $36.00
Total for all 4 workers = $136.80
Note: Workers A and C received the guaranteed minimum 4 hours pay each.

www.ingramcontent.com/pod-product-compliance
Lightning Source LLC
Chambersburg PA
CBHW080738230426
43665CB00020B/2785